CANON LAW AS MINISTRY:

FREEDOM AND GOOD ORDER FOR THE CHURCH

CANON LAW AS MINISTRY: FREEDOM AND GOOD ORDER FOR THE CHURCH

James A. Coriden

PAULIST PRESS
New York/Mahwah, N.J.

Cover design by Lisa Buckley

Book design by Theresa M. Sparacio

Library of Congress Cataloging-in-Publication Data

Coriden, James A.
    Canon law as ministry : freedom and good order for the church / by James A. Coriden.
        p.   cm.
    Includes bibliographical references and index.
    ISBN 0-8091-3978-2 (alk. paper)
    1. Canon law. I. Title.

LAW+
262.9′01—dc21

00-042763

Published by Paulist Press
997 Macarthur Boulevard
Mahwah, New Jersey 07430

www.paulistpress.com

Printed and bound in the
United States of America

CONTENTS

ABBREVIATIONS   ix

INTRODUCTION   1
The Ministry of Canon Law   1
An Overview of the Contents   2
Those for Whom the Book Was Written   3
Personal Notes   4
Style and Usage   5

CHAPTER 1: THE DEBATE ABOUT THE NATURE OF CANON LAW   7
Causes of the Identity Crisis   8
Viewpoints and Perspectives   11
Seven Schools of Thought   13
For the Future: A Ministerial Vision   19

CHAPTER 2: ABOUT ROOTS AND NAMES AND HISTORY   21
Rules in the New Testament   21
What's in a Name?   27
A Look Back at History   28

CHAPTER 3: A VISION OF CHURCH:
THE THEOLOGICAL CONTEXT FOR THE MINISTRY   33
Point of Departure: Local Church   34
Communities of Word and Sacrament   37

The Action of the Holy Spirit 38
Communion 41
The People of God 48
Mission 50
The Body of Christ 52
A Sacrament of Salvation 53
Apostolic 56
One Church: A Single Complex Reality 59

CHAPTER 4: CHURCHES IN PLACE:
THE SITUATIONAL CONTEXT FOR THE MINISTRY 61
Particularities of Place: Elements 63
Particularities of Place: Principles 75

CHAPTER 5: FREEDOM IN THE CHURCH:
FIRST FOCUS OF THE MINISTRY OF THE CANONIST 79
Freedom in Christ 80
Religious Freedom 83
Primacy of Conscience 86
Power of Discretion 89
Discernment of the Spirit 91
Rights of Persons and Communities 95
Inculturation 100
Churches as Voluntary Associations 102

CHAPTER 6: GOOD ORDER IN THE CHURCH:
SECOND FOCUS OF THE CANONICAL MINISTRY 106
Power Language in Canon Law 107
Sources of Power in the New Testament 107
The Scope of Christ's Authority 109
Authority as Service 111
Distortions of Authority 114
The Second Vatican Council on Authority 118
Hierarchy: Concept and Reality 120
Authority as Participative 122
Laypersons and the Power of Governance 125

CHAPTER 7: CANON LAW AS MINISTRY   132
What Canonists Do   132
The Gift of Good Guidance   134
What Is a Ministry?   135
Change and Control   136
Canon Law Related to Other Disciplines   139
Canon Law and Other Ministries   146
Canon Law as a Science   150
Education for Canonical Ministry   154
Jesus on the Hazards of the Ministry   157

AN URGENT AGENDA FOR THE FUTURE OF THE MINISTRY   159
Ongoing Canonical Revision   159
Diversity of Discipline   163
Canonical Creativity   167

NOTES   174
BIBLIOGRAPHY   188
INDEX   199

ABBREVIATIONS

AAS   *Acta Apostolicae Sedis*

c, cc   canon, canons

CCEO   *Codex Canonum Ecclesiarum Orientalium*, Code of Canons of the Eastern Churches, promulgated by Pope John Paul II, October 18, 1990

CIC   *Codex Iuris Canonici*, Code of Canon Law, promulgated by Pope John Paul II, January 25, 1983

CLD   *Canon Law Digest*, Officially Published Documents Affecting the Code of Canon Law, 11 vols. Ed. T. L. Bouscaren, J. I. O'Connor, E. Pfnausch. Milwaukee: Bruce, 1934; Washington, D.C.: CLSA, 1991.

DOCUMENTS OF THE SECOND VATICAN COUNCIL

AA   *Apostolicam actuositatem*, Decree on the Apostolate of the Laity, November 18, 1965

AG   *Ad gentes divinitas*, Decree on the Missionary Activity of the Church, December 7, 1965

CD   *Christus Dominus*, Decree on the Pastoral Office of Bishops in the Church, October 28, 1965

DH   *Dignitatis humanae*, Declaration on Religious Freedom, December 7, 1965

DV   *Dei verbum,* Dogmatic Constitution on Divine Revelation, November 18, 1965

GS   *Gaudium et spes,* Pastoral Constitution on the Church in the World of Today, December 6, 1965

LG   *Lumen Gentium,* Dogmatic Constitution on the Church, November 21, 1964

NA   *Nostra aetate,* Declaration on the Church's Relation to Non-Christian Religions, October 28, 1965

OE   *Orientalium ecclesiarum,* Decree on the Eastern Catholic Churches, November 21, 1964

OT   *Optatam totius,* Decree on Priestly Formation, October 28, 1965

PO   *Presbyterorum ordinis,* Decree on the Ministry and Life of Priests, December 7, 1965

SC   *Sacrosanctum concilium,* Constitution on the Sacred Liturgy, December 4, 1963

UR   *Unitatis redintegratio,* Decree on Ecumenism, November 21, 1964

INTRODUCTION

THE PURPOSE OF THIS BOOK is to portray a vision of canonical ministry in the present and for the future. The book attempts to describe the ministry of canonists within its indispensable settings: a theology of the church and a consciousness of local churches in place. It examines the particular goals of this ministry: Christian freedom and good order. The book compares the canonical ministry with other prominent church ministries and situates it within the other theological disciplines. It concludes with an urgent agenda for the future.

THE MINISTRY OF CANON LAW

"Canon Law" names the system of rules which governs the Roman Catholic Church. It is a very ancient system, nearly two thousand years old. The earliest collections of canons were made in the second and third centuries. Canon Law developed into a science, an academic field of study with recognized principles and methods, in the twelfth century. Since that time, church leaders and distinguished scholars have generated a vast body of refined canonical literature. So "Canon Law" describes a system of rules for the church, an area of academic study, and a body of scientific literature. But with equal accuracy "Canon Law"

1

names a vital and long-standing *ministry* within the church. This book is about that professional ministry.

This is not a "how to" book. That is, it does not attempt to describe the attitudes, procedures, methods, tactics, or skills needed to practice the canonical ministry. Rather it sets forth guidelines for the ministry, the markers of its trajectories, the pylons for its dynamic function.

Canon Law is a ministry performed within the church and on behalf of those who are the church. It is practiced by those who have been prepared for this ministry, who have learned not only the canonical rules but the canonical profession. The practice of the profession involves both a knowledge of the canons and an understanding of what they mean to the life of the community. This includes the sensitivity and skill to explain, adapt, and apply rules fairly for the benefit of God's people.

The church and its ministries face a new situation today, a different world, with new "postmodern" challenges. The church is slowly and painfully coming to terms with its new identity as a true "world church" rather than a "European religious export." It is engaged in a critical struggle for its own inculturation. This new situation poses creative challenges to the canonical ministry, the vital ministry of the church's guidance and governance.

Canonists, like the churches they serve, stand facing the brightness of a new century which is also the beginning of the third millennium of Christian history. The moment compels them to examine "the signs of the times" with a vision illumined by both the perennial glow of the Christian scriptures and the fresh light of the Second Vatican Council.

AN OVERVIEW OF THE CONTENTS

Most specifically, then, this book is about the *ministry* of canonists, the *essential contexts for* the ministry, and the *specific focuses of* that ministry.

First, the extended postconciliar debate about the nature of

Canon Law and the variety of viewpoints in that debate set the scene for the rest of the book (chapter 1).

This is followed by a brief look back at the New Testament origins of the ministry, at its peculiar nomenclature, and at some examples of the historical functions it has served (chapter 2).

There are two essential contexts for the canonical ministry, theological and situational. The ministry must always be guided by a balanced and accurate theology of the church, and it must never lose sight of its "locality," the specific actuality of its communities in place and time (chapters 3 and 4).

The practice of the ministry strives to achieve two main goals for its communities: genuine Christian freedom and good order. These twin goals and overarching purposes give focus to the canonical ministry (chapters 5 and 6).

These four chapters (3 through 6) on the context and focus of canonical ministry are the heart of the book. The elements and themes that comprise them are drawn almost exclusively from two sources: the New Testament and the Second Vatican Council.

Then the canonical ministry itself is examined. This includes the actual functions of the ministry, its Pauline parallel in First Corinthians, its relationships to other disciplines and other ministries, its educational preparation, and the perils associated with it (chapter 7).

The book concludes with three specific proposals for the future, three examples of issues which need urgent attention as canonical ministers look ahead.

THOSE FOR WHOM THE BOOK WAS WRITTEN

The author of this book hopes to engage other canonists, first of all, in a reflection on their own ministry. Those preparing for the ministry or considering this ministerial specialization should engage in this same reflective process. Similarly, those who employ, support, or relate to canonists will benefit from these pages. Could it be that its message will make a much misunderstood ministry better appreciated?

Those engaged in or preparing for other ministries in the Roman Catholic communion will profit from this analysis of the canonical ministry. Most of what is set forth here also sheds light on the ministries of preaching, teaching, liturgical celebration, and church administration.

Although the context for this study is the Roman Catholic Church, those in the ministries of leadership and governance in other Christian churches may find it of interest and value. The ecclesial vision sketched here is consciously ecumenical, but the church orders that embody that vision vary in the different traditions.

Those committed to the life of the churches—theologians, ministers, and other thoughtful believers—might be stimulated by this discussion of a uniquely influential strain of the Catholic tradition.

PERSONAL NOTES

The author has been engaged in the study and teaching of Canon Law as well as the practice of canonical ministry for well over forty years. Yet these reflections are aimed at the future, not at the past. They depict a vision of hope, replete with deep-set values, which will reveal a working plan for the years to come. At least that is the author's intent.

Historical perspective is always necessary, and one might expect a history of Canon Law, at least in summary form, in such a book. However, I attempted such a historical summary in *An Introduction to Canon Law* (New York/Mahwah, N.J.: Paulist Press, 1990, pp. 9–29) and did not feel the need to insert something similar here. Several excellent historical studies are included in the bibliography.

I thank the Washington Theological Union community, my academic home for twenty-five years, for its continual encouragement and support, especially in the form of sabbatical and academic leaves for study. I gratefully acknowledge a grant from the Louisville Institute in support of research on this project during parts of 1997 and 1998.

I "road-tested" some of the central ideas in this book at four distinguished faculties of Canon Law: The Catholic University of America, Washington, D.C. (September 30, 1997); the Pontifical Gregorian University, Rome (October 30, 1997); Saint Paul University, Ottawa (March 20, 1998); and the Pontifical University of the Holy Cross, Rome (April 22, 1999). On each occasion the response was valuable, and I remain grateful to them for their reactions well as for the gracious hospitality accorded to me.

STYLE AND USAGE

The author has sought to minimize the use of footnotes by leaving single biblical and conciliar citations in parentheses within the text. Only when citations are multiple or their repetition becomes visually cumbersome are they placed in footnotes.

The designation of *church* (in lower case) means local church (e.g., parish), or particular church (e.g., diocese), or the church "universal." Only when it means quite specifically the Roman Catholic Church is the word capitalized.

"St. Mary's on Main Street" stands for a local congregation in all its concreteness and particularity. Churches are essentially local, even as they are always catholic, within a larger communion, and St. Mary's is used to underscore that reality. St. Mary's, in the author's mind, bears some resemblance to his home parish, St. Joseph's Church on Hohman Street in Hammond, Indiana.

The metaphors of garden, park, and forest for the church and the churches are invoked because of what they convey about life, growth, change, and the mutual interdependence of their elements, as with the vine and the branches.

CHAPTER 1

THE DEBATE ABOUT THE NATURE

OF CANON LAW

A TRULY REMARKABLE DEBATE about the nature of Canon Law has raged in the decades since the close of the Second Vatican Council. This protracted and profound discussion has been called "a radical crisis" for Canon Law because it involves basic questions about the very nature and function of Canon Law.

Leading canonical scholars around the world have engaged in this lively discussion. They have not resorted to anger or vitriol; the debate has been civil and learned. Nevertheless disagreements are deep-seated and wide-ranging, and the debated questions profound. What is Canon Law? Is it a juridical or a theological science? What is its proper scope? Is Canon Law about the regulation of word and sacrament, or about church-state relations? What is canonical methodology? Are questions answered by legal reasoning or by theological argument? Such questions go to the very identity of Canon Law.

One notable characteristic of this more-than-thirty-year debate has been its academic abstractness. It has been carried on almost entirely at the level of pure theory. The vast literature generated in the discussion—a dozen books and scores of scholarly articles—is almost entirely devoid of illustrations, concrete applications, or practical consequences. In other words, the discussion most often does not reach the point of practice.

However, the outcome of the debate will have profound implications in the long term. Indeed, the results will shape Canon Law, the exercise of authority and the extent of freedom in the church, and the very face of the church itself. The issues involve the nature of rule-making, rights of participation, and the church's ability to adapt in different times and cultural situations. The consequences of this "academic conversation" will be far-reaching and drastic.

So far the folks down at St. Mary's on Main Street have been blissfully unaware of this controversy about the nature of Canon Law. Even most practicing canonists, as they toil in diocesan tribunals or administrative offices, have not yet felt the effects of this radical debate concerning the nature of their "science." It has been a lively conversation about serious concerns, but it has not yet had much effect on canonical practice or life in the church. That will soon change. The results of this discussion will have major ramifications for the future of the church, affecting not only the quality of life within its local communities, but also the fulfillment of its mission in the world.

This chapter will examine: 1) what occasioned the postconciliar debate, 2) viewpoints and perspectives in the debate, 3) seven schools of thought within the debate, and 4) a ministerial vision for the future.

CAUSES OF THE IDENTITY CRISIS

Several factors gave rise to this extended debate about the identity of Canon Law.

The Code Revision Process

The *aggiornamento* (bringing up to date) of the *Code of Canon Law* announced by Pope John XXIII in 1959 really began in 1965, as the Vatican Council concluded. The process continued until the publication of the revised *Code* in 1983. It was intended to be much more than a simple updating or revision; Pope John actually called it a *recognitio*, that is, a rethinking or reunderstanding of the *Code*. This search for a new understanding of Canon Law caused a reexamination of the very nature of the discipline.

The revisionary enterprise surfaced basic differences regarding the need for church law, the nature of that law in an ecclesial body, and the wisdom of its arrangement in a code. The "codification" of the church's rules was first attempted in 1904, and resulted in the *Code* of 1917. In previous centuries the church was well served by "collections" of canons. The process and the results of codifying the canons has been criticized as abstract and ahistorical.

The scope and extent of the postconciliar "rethinking" of Canon Law was narrowed drastically by the Commission's initial decision to begin each subcommittee's work by using the 1917 *Code* as the point of departure. That choice changed the task. It became more a redrafting of the existing rules to conform to the Council documents than a thoroughgoing revision of the church's canonical system. In other words, the debate about the deeper issues of the nature of Canon Law was deliberately set aside in order to accomplish the more pragmatic goal of producing as new code of canons.

Some of the canonists in the postconciliar debate were also major players in the revision process itself, for example, Klaus Mörsdorf, William Bertrams, Peter Lombardía, and Peter Huizing. These scholars were compelled to put aside their deep theological and philosophical differences about the nature of Canon Law in order to accomplish the task at hand. In other words, the debate was prolonged because the time was not yet ripe for its resolution.

The Ecclesiology of the Vatican Council

Another and even more profound reason for the debate was the astonishingly new and deeper self-understanding which the church achieved in the Council itself. Pope John XXIII intuited that the Council would have a major impact on Canon Law and for that reason he linked the two, an ecumenical council and the updating of the *Code,* in one dramatic announcement on January 25, 1959.

The intense struggles over the Dogmatic Constitution on the Church *(Lumen Gentium)* resulted in a renewed theological vision of the nature of the church. This unanticipated development was the Council's central achievement. However, upon closer analysis, the documents of the Council actually reveal two distinct ecclesiologies, one of sacrament and communion, the other of a juridically organized "perfect society" which parallels the structure of secular states. The duality reflects the unresolved tensions at the Council.

Eventually *"communio* ecclesiology" emerged as a superior and unified theological vision which now dominates Catholic thinking about the church. However, this theological development raised significant questions about Canon Law. The canonical tradition contains such a residue of the old "perfect society" thought and content that it seems ill-suited to this postconciliar vision of the church. For example, the *Code* ascribes to the papal office the authority of a virtually absolute monarch while affording minimal expression to episcopal collegiality. In sum, many canonical provisions adopted after the Council did not incorporate the authentic theological vision which emerged from the Council, namely *"communio* ecclesiology."

The Negative Image of Canon Law

Another cause of the present debate also stemmed from the Council. The conciliar discussions included a rather negative assessment of Canon Law and "canon lawyers." Legalism was denounced by the Council fathers along with triumphalism and clericalism.[1] A rigidly juridical mode of church leadership was viewed as unsuitable and detrimental. This negative judgment about the effects of Canon Law on the life of the church led to some disaffection with the discipline as well as to its reassessment.

Laws in a Community of Love?

A fourth contributing factor to the debate was a continuation of the troubling accusation made against Canon Law at the outset of the twentieth century by the distinguished Protestant historian of church order, Rudolf Sohm (1841–1917). Sohm argued trenchantly and persistently that Canon Law was alien, even contrary, to the very notion of what a Christian church is.[2] He said that a community of love cannot be a community of laws. "The essence of Canon Law is in contradiction to the essence of the church."[3]

Sohm's argument with Catholicism echoes the claims of reformers through the centuries that the church has become overly juridicized and distanced from the gospels. As recently as 1973 the eminent theologian of the church, Yves Congar, wrote an important article entitled "Rudolph Sohm Still Questions Us."[4] Many of the participants in the debate about the identity of Canon Law still refer to Sohm's writings and attempt to respond to his allegations.

VIEWPOINTS AND PERSPECTIVES

The long-standing debate about the nature and identity of Canon Law has engaged many contemporary canonical writers. Those involved in the dialogue include some of the most learned and respected scholars from Canon Law faculties around the world. Their debate is not two-sided, but multi-sided. It is a discussion with many points of view, often referred to as "schools of thought."

These perspectives are not necessarily mutually exclusive or contradictory, any more than are the viewpoints of those standing at different places on a mountainside. The view of a person higher up on the mountain does not exclude or contradict that of one standing a little lower. It is a matter of scope and perspective, a broader or narrower outlook. Furthermore, these views of Canon Law often shade into one another, they are complementary, overlapping, and their distinctions one from another are not always clear. The differing views are greatly affected by the context of their proponents, just as political opinions often differ depending on whether the proponent is in or out of office.

Some authors teach in schools of civil law (e.g., in Italian universities), and they constantly compare and contrast their views with their secular-law colleagues. Some authors teach in countries wherein concordats between the government and the Holy See make Canon Law of considerable civil import, for example, in marriage and divorce, in financial support for the church. Many other canonists live and work where there is separation between church and state, and for them Canon Law functions almost exclusively within the church.

Several canonical writers are members of the personal prelature "Opus Dei," and are conditioned by that association, its spirituality, and its unique loyalties. Still others are engaged in the formation of candidates for church ministry, in seminaries or schools of theology, and their views are shaped by that work.

Some canonists have a slight theological background or learned their theology before the Council and never fully adapted to a renewed ecclesiology. Frequently students absorb the views of their own teachers on the faculty where they studied; consequently many remain loyal disciples of their "magisters."

Often canonists aspire to higher offices in the church, and their expression of opinion is nuanced to please (or at least not displease) those in authority. It also happens that those employed by the church or agencies within it are on occasion unwilling to criticize the views of their employers.

As is always the case, theories and viewpoints are colored by personal context. Everyone's perspective is deeply affected by his or her personal situation and the "temper of the times." The Apostle Paul, Dietrich Bonhoeffer, and Martin Luther King, Jr., all wrote powerful works while imprisoned, and their situations conditioned their writings.[5] Many Catholic theologians who wrote in the first fifteen years after the Second Vatican Council did so with candor, imagination, and openness, and without the caution, fear, and self-censorship which characterized many in earlier and later periods.

SEVEN SCHOOLS OF THOUGHT

There are at least seven discernible points of view or "schools of thought" in the contemporary debate about the nature of Canon Law:[6]

The Public Ecclesiastical Law School

These scholars take "juridicity" as their starting point. They view Canon Law as a juridical system just like the legal systems in secular societies, except that it is located within the unique society *(sui generis)* which is the church. Their basic premise is that wherever there is a human society there is a legal system *(ubi societas ibi ius)*. Wherever there is social interaction, intersubjectivity, there are rights and duties. This applies to a bridge club as well as to the United Nations. This theory conformed well to the vision of the church as a "juridically perfect society," meaning a society which possesses all the juridic means to pursue its end, its own common good. These authors strive to keep Canon Law as a respectable legal science on a par with other legal systems. In some countries it is taught in state universities under the rubric of "ecclesiastical law." These professors do not deny the spiritual purposes of the church and its canonical system, but they say that the spiritual realities lie outside the juridical realm. Such realities as the Holy Spirit, grace, charity, divine law, and the salvation of souls *(salus animarum suprema lex)* are "meta-juridical," that is, they are above and beyond the scope of legal system. The method for interpreting or applying Canon Law is purely juridical, the same as in any other legal system. Canon Law is an autonomous juridical science, independent of theology; it is a division or subset of legal studies.

This view, sometimes referred to as the Roman school of *ius publicum ecclesiasticum,* is especially associated with the laymen and laywomen who teach in Italian state universities.[7]

The Opus Dei School

These writers envision Canon Law as an autonomous science, as does the previous group, but they emphasize its complete dependence on ecclesiastical authority. Canon Law is a legal system like any other, and its methodology is purely juridical, but its legislation and interpretations are entirely subject to the church's authority. For these proponents Canon Law is a species of the genus law, and therefore independent of the science of theology, although it is closely related to and strongly influenced by ecclesiology, for example, the notion of the church as the people of God. For them Canon Law represents the juridic dimension of the people of God.

These canonists view Canon Law as the ordering structure of the church, the source of its internal justice, the instrument of its just social order. Divine law and human law together form a single juridic structure, the canonical order *(ordenamiento canonico).* It is a juridical vision, but one conscious of and sensitive to its theological setting, that is, within the mystery that is the church, the people of God.

This viewpoint is attributed to the Canon Law faculties related to Opus Dei, namely those at the University of Navarra in Pamplona, Spain, and the Pontifical University of the Holy Cross in Rome.[8]

The Munich School

These authors maintain that Canon Law is truly a sacred science, a theological discipline, but with a methodology that is juridical. Theology and Canon Law are not only closely linked, but form an organic unity, differentiated only by the methods used within each. The question of the nature and mission of the church has priority; the question of the place and organization of Canon Law within the church is subsequent. Canon Law has a supernatural foundation because it is based on the mystery of the church founded by Jesus Christ. This law is the order of the community of the new people of God.

The school acknowledges that the church is a society, which, like any other, must have a legal system *(ubi societas ibi ius),* and in this sense there is an analogical similarity between Canon Law and civil law. However, Canon Law is not a species of the genus law, because it is grounded in an identity which is primarily theological.

The church proclaims salvation through both word and sacrament; these two inseparable realities are the sources of the church's life. Both word and sacrament have a juridic aspect, because they were *commanded* by the Lord (e.g., Mk 16, 15–16: "Go into the whole world and proclaim the gospel....Whoever believes and is baptized will be saved") and the church is *bound to obey.* The task of Canon Law is to regulate this juridic aspect of the church.

The church on the local level is a true, apostolic communion of word and sacrament, and the communion of churches *(communio ecclesiarum)* on the universal level is the word and sacrament of Christ. Interpersonal relations and structural articulations characterize both levels of the people of God as human communities, and Canon Law provides their normative organization.

Using Thomas Aquinas' classic definition of law as "an ordination of reason for the common good promulgated by the one who has care of the community,"[9] they substitute *ordinatio fidei* for *ordinatio rationis,* meaning that the church belongs to the order of faith rather than that of reason. Therefore the church's law is an ordering directed by faith to the end of the church which is communion *(communio).* "Communion" is that complex theological reality which includes both a graced relationship with God and the mutual relations between members and local congregations within the church. Communion is the formal principle of canon law. At this point "law" or the juridical science is purely auxiliary to Canon Law, it is used in a subordinate way, as rhetoric is employed in the preaching of the gospel.[10]

The Roman Curia School

These canonists assert that the church is a human society elevated to the supernatural sphere; its internal, ontological structure can only be actualized and manifested in its external, sociojuridic structure, as the human soul is given expression in a physical body. This view is based on a philosophical anthropology, a variation on the hylomorphic theory of matter and form. Canon Law is part of the external structure of the church which makes visible and operative its internal, spiritual, and salvific nature. The church's internal nature and mission are expressed externally in its organized social unity (unio socialis indolis organizatoriae). Canon Law is one of the church's pastoral means or instruments which serves its divinely ordained end: the salvation of the faithful.

Since juridic activity is specified by the end which it serves, Canon Law is only analogically, not univocally, like secular law. Canon Law is theological, its authority is sacramental. The Holy Spirit and the created gifts of faith, hope, and charity are bestowed in baptism, and the rights derived from baptism can be exercised only within communion. In this metaphysical vision ecclesial communion (communio ecclesialis) is identified with the church's sociojuridical element.[11]

The Concilium Project

Some authors acknowledge a relationship between Canon Law and theology, but they wish to reconfigure that relationship. They call for an end to the absolutizing effect of giving too much theological weight to canonical structures, for example, the college of cardinals or the plenitude of papal power, by considering them to be "of divine law." They ask that Canon Law shift from its preoccupation with the church's autonomy and authority vis-à-vis the state and return to its original role as the normative articulation of the church's sacramental nature.

In a historical perspective the community's rules were once sacramental, that is, the rights and duties of its members related to the celebration of baptism and the Eucharist. Then, as offices (especially the monarchical episcopacy and the papacy) developed, the rules focused more on official authority, parallel to that exercised by secular powers. Now it is time, these canonists believe, to reverse this trend, and center the church's rules once again on its sacramental realities.

The church is the sacrament of the intimate union with God, the visible sacrament of the saving unity of those who regard Jesus as source of salvation. At the same time the sacraments are the fundamental organic structure of the church, and Canon Law exists to regulate the sacramental life of those incorporated into the church through baptism and brought into full communion through participation in the Eucharist. The canons are to give expression to the structures of the *communio* which is the church.

Canon Law is a theological science, one entirely subject to faith and the church's convictions about itself and its pastoral needs.[12]

The School of Values

These canonical writers see theology and Canon Law as organically connected, with theology ruling over and sitting in judgment on the adequacy of canonical enactments. The task of theology is to perceive, articulate, and explain God's revelation, and to lead the Christian community to enunciate its faith and its values. For example, theology teaches about the ecumenical imperative to restore Christian unity. The task of Canon Law is to produce rules for action, norms for the attainment of Christian values, for example, guidelines to enable and encourage ecumenical activity. The object of theology is knowledge, the object of Canon Law is action.

This position is based on Bernard Lonergan's cognitional theory, and focuses on the distinctly different functions of theology and Canon Law: faith seeking understanding as over against faith seeking action. Both are rooted in faith; the canons attempt to elicit or direct action by the community of faithful in pursuit of its own values. For example, theological deliberations at the Council reached a new understanding of episcopal collegiality, and canonists found new structures, like the Synod of Bishops and episcopal conferences, to express that theological insight. The rules or structures enacted for this purpose are never to be confused with the underlying mysteries.

This theory stresses the horizons or fields of vision of those who make and interpret laws. The post–Vatican II canonical horizon is distinctly different from those which preceded it, and a new attitude of mind *(novus habitus mentis)* is demanded to function within it.[13]

The Institutional School

Some contemporary canonists distinguish between an underlying "institutional law," an original, fundamental, and structural reality, and the positive canonical norms built upon it at any given time. They see a set of

> fundamental elements of the hierarchical and organic structure of the church as established by its Divine Founder, based upon apostolic or other most ancient tradition, as well as the principal norms concerning the exercise of the threefold office entrusted to the church[14]

as defining a kind of basic constitution of the church. Other "rules and norms of action" or positive statutes are added when needed, as, for example, in the 1983 *Code* revision.

This "pre-positive institutional law" is not considered to be "divine law" exactly, but it comes close. It is attributed partially to the intention of Christ or the action of the Spirit (and hence is sometimes called "revealed"), but partially to "most ancient tradition" as well. It forms a core juridical structure which grounds and justifies the entire canonical order.

The precise content of this institutional core is difficult to specify, but it includes the sacraments; the teaching, sanctifying, and pastoring functions; and the gifts and ministries needed to build up the community. Everything else is the product of human wisdom: rules issued by ecclesiastical legislators, that is, councils, popes, bishops, religious chapters.

These two factors, fundamental elements and rules of action, taken together, make up the church's juridical order. For example, the sacraments of Christian initiation are a fundamental Christian reality, and the standards regarding the age of confirmation are specifications for the reception of the sacrament.[15]

These brief summaries cannot do justice to the carefully articulated and nuanced theories of these "schools" and their individual authors about the nature of Canon Law and its relationship to theology. However, they convey some sense of the reasoned positions in the debate.

Obviously this discussion is not about "right" or "wrong" theories, but about different points of view. Most of the viewpoints are relatively close together, with differing stances, approaches, and emphases. Still, some provide more realistic vantage points for practical church governance, while other theories offer more satisfying theological explanations and raise fewer problems. Some more fully incorporate an authentic, contemporary ecclesiology.

FOR THE FUTURE: A MINISTERIAL VISION

The debate about the identity of Canon Law seems to be reaching a resolution as the church enters a new millennium. A unifying consensus is emerging, and one major purpose of this book is to describe that consensus and contribute to it.

However, the foregoing theoretical stances or "schools of thought" are principally concerned with Canon Law as a science, as a body of literature, as a field of study, and not about Canon Law as it is practiced.

The discussion might be compared to an examination of the legal profession where one would consider the laws made by legislatures and the decisions of the courts, but overlook what lawyers actually *do* for a living. Or, in observing the medical profession, it would be like deducing the art of healing from the sciences of biology, chemistry, and physiology, without considering medical *practice* itself. It would give a very partial and distorted view of what doctors and nurses actually *do* in caring for patients.

The kernel of this book's thesis is that Canon Law is primarily a ministry in the church. It is a specialization within ministry, and finds its identity within the communion called church. Canon Law is a species or subset within the genus of ecclesial ministry, not a species within the genus of law or lawyering.

Canon Law is a vital ministry in the life of the church's communities. Canon Law is also an academic discipline, an ancient tradition, and even a sacred science. But what is essential to grasp and hold is that Canon Law's primary identity is that of a church ministry. As a ministry Canon Law is grounded in theology, yet adapted to the pastoral needs of God's people in specific places and times, under the guidance of God's Spirit. It stands for the freedom of the faithful and strives for good order in their communities as it embodies Christ's authority as service.

CHAPTER 2

ABOUT ROOTS AND NAMES AND HISTORY

WHEN BEGINNING A SEARCH, it is first necessary to get one's bearings, to ascertain and comprehend one's relative position. In searching for the identity of Canon Law as a ministry, it is necessary to look back to the origins of the church, to understand the names given to rules within the church's life, and to glimpse a few historic milestones or trail markers. This brief chapter explores these three steps: 1) rules found within the New Testament literature, 2) the names chosen for the church's rules, and 3) some historic turnings which have shaped the canonical ministry.

RULES IN THE NEW TESTAMENT

What kinds of rules about life in the earliest communities would one expect to find in the church's founding documents? Rules for good order emerged very early. Here are four examples: a) the conciliar decision-making of Acts 15, b) the conflict resolution of Matthew 18, c) the instruction on the use of the Spirit's gifts in 1 Corinthians 12–14, and d) the qualifications for leadership in the Pastoral Letters.

Decision-making

A critical dispute of major proportions arose in the earliest church. It is well documented in the Acts of the Apostles (15) and in Paul's letter to the Galatians (2).

> Some men came down to Antioch from Judea and began to teach the brothers: "Unless you are circumcised according to Mosaic practice, you cannot be saved." This created dissension and much controversy between them and Paul and Barnabas. (Acts 15, 1–2)

At issue was the very identity of the new community of the followers of Jesus. Did its new members have to become Jews in order to join the disciples of Christ? Did the men have to undergo circumcision and did everyone have to obey the Jewish dietary laws as necessary steps on their journey of conversion to "Christianity"? These questions went right to the core of the new church's self-understanding.

The problem arose in Antioch, but it was solved in Jerusalem. Those who said that circumcision was necessary for salvation caused dissension within the church at Antioch, which included both Jews and Gentiles. Thus Paul and Barnabas and others traveled to Jerusalem where they met with the apostles and presbyters to decide the matter.

The debate was prolonged. Peter spoke about God's gift of the Holy Spirit to the Gentiles. Paul and Barnabas told of the signs and wonders God had worked among the Gentiles. However, it was James, the leader of the Jerusalem church, who suggested a solution: we ought not to cause difficulties for the Gentiles who have turned to God.

The apostles and presbyters, in agreement with the whole church of Jerusalem, decided to send representatives with Paul and Barnabas back to Antioch with this message:

> It is the decision of the Holy Spirit and of us not to place on you any other burden beyond these necessities, namely to abstain from meat sacrificed to idols, from blood, from meats of strangled animals, and from unlawful marriage.[1] If

you keep free of these, you will be doing what is right. (Acts 15, 28-29)

In addition to the basic decision itself, which meant that Christian converts did not have to first become converts to Judaism, four aspects of Luke's portrayal of this "council of Jerusalem" and its crucial decision are important to note: a) that the decision was made "in council," that is, in a gathering of the apostles and elders, after considerable debate; this became the "conciliar" or "synodical" pattern for future decision-making in the church; b) that those who made the decision were conscious of being in agreement with the whole of the local church and with the Holy Spirit of God; c) that minimal burdens were to be imposed and maximum freedom of action permitted; and d) that the ritual matters which were mentioned as necessary (because they were important to those of Jewish background at the time) did not become parts of the enduring tradition.

The resolution of this dispute provided the most influential paradigm for disciplinary decision-making in the history of the church.

Conflict Resolution

Matthew's gospel (18, 15-20) contains a three-step process for dealing with personal disputes or "conflict resolution," which is also paradigmatic for Christian communities.

1) If one member of the community commits an offensive act against another, the one offended should go and speak one-to-one with the alleged offender.
2) If that personal confrontation or attempt at reconciliation does not succeed, then another member or two of the community should be brought in as witnesses or as mediators.
3) That failing, the matter should be brought before the entire local church, and that assembly is empowered to reconcile or dismiss the offender.

The process has roots in the Jewish legal tradition (Dt 19, 15), but it probably also reflects the actual practice of Matthew's church when dealing with those who did not abide by community standards or gave offense in serious matters.

The gospel passage attributes great authority to the local community of the faithful, because of the presence of the Lord Jesus in their midst: "For where two or three are gathered together in my name, there am I in the midst of them" (Mt 18, 20). The same rationale applies today. Christ is present in the Christian assembly through his Holy Spirit. The process described by Matthew in the words of Jesus provides a classic pattern for conflict resolution and reconciliation within the Christian community.

Use of the Spirit's Gifts

The church at Corinth was quite young when Paul wrote his first letter to that community. Paul had lived in Corinth for a year and a half, and he first wrote to them, in about the year 54, a few years after he had departed from there. Factions and dissension had arisen, and abuses in personal conduct and in community worship had been reported to Paul. He addressed the issues forcefully in an attempt to correct the thinking and the behavior of the members of the Corinthian community.

One problem involved the gifts *(charismata)* of the Holy Spirit (1 Cor 12–14), for example, speaking in tongues, interpretation of tongues, discernment of spirits, prophecy, or healing, and their manifestations when the community gathered for worship. Their undisciplined use occasioned confusion in the assembly. "If the whole church meets in one place and everyone speaks in tongues," if outsiders should come in, "will they not say that you are out of your minds?" (14, 23).

Paul wrote an exquisite instruction on the gifts of the Spirit, employing some of the most beautiful imagery in all of biblical literature:

> The body is one and has many members, but all the members, many though they are, are one body, and so it is with

Christ....If one member suffers, all the members suffer with it; if one member is honored, all the members share its joy. You, then, are the body of Christ.

If I speak with human tongues and angelic as well, but do not have love, I am a noisy gong, a clanging cymbal....Love is patient; love is kind....Love never fails....There are in the end three things that last: faith, hope, and love, and the greatest of these is love. (1 Cor 12 and 13)

Paul then offered practical directions on the use of the gifts in their assemblies (14, 26–40). His general principle is: "Everything should be done for building up" (26b). The upbuilding of the community is paramount. To that end, "everything must be done properly and in good order" (40), because "God is not a God of disorder, but of peace" (33). Ours is a God of peace, and the tranquillity of order is proper to assemblies held in his name.

Paul went on to give very explicit instructions: "When you assemble, one has a psalm, another some instruction to give, still another a revelation to share; one speaks in a tongue, another interprets" (26a). Remarkably, he claimed that his directions, which amount to a detailed order of worship, were from the Lord: "what I am writing to you is a commandment of the Lord" (37b). Yet this order of prayer has not endured unchanged in the church's practice.[2] As in the case of the policy for Gentile converts, even though decided in solemn assembly, the church's confidence about the Spirit's guidance permitted subsequent changes in practice.[3]

Qualifications for Leaders

Some of the letters attributed to Paul are designated as "pastoral" because they were addressed to the pastoral leaders of the local churches rather than to the churches themselves. These contain explicit and detailed qualifications for certain church offices. Those for bishops (*episkopoi*, overseers) and deacons (*diakonoi*) are detailed in 1 Timothy (3, 2–13) and those for elders (*presbyteroi*) in Titus (1, 5–10). For example:

As I instructed you, a presbyter must be irreproachable, married only once, the father of children who are believers and are known not to be wild and insubordinate. (Ti 1, 5–6)

The patterns and contents of the lists of qualifications are quite similar, and although they may have derived from a common source, none has been discovered.

Such statements of desirable personal qualities for candidates for church ministries have been a central feature of church rule-making ever since the time of the Pastorals. Indeed, nothing could be more appropriate than for the church to set standards and expectations for those designated to minister in its name.

Some of the specific qualifications contained in these early lists might strike contemporary Catholics as dramatically unfamiliar: "married only once, good managers of his household, keeping his children under control" (1 Tm 3, 2 and 4). These qualities sound strange to those conditioned to a celibate clergy. Other qualifications are more predictable: of true faith, a good teacher, gentle, not arrogant or aggressive, not greedy or a drunkard, of good repute. There is a reliance on the classical virtues: moderation, justice, devotion, self-control. Women seem to be included among the deacons (1 Tm 3, 11).

The church's criteria for its ministers have changed in important ways since the Pastorals were written, yet there have been strong elements of continuity as well. The requirements for leaders of Christian communities remain largely the same, while different times and cultures have called for different personal qualities in those who assume these roles, for example, the monastic models of prayer and celibate lifestyle.

These four examples from the New Testament, viewed in retrospect, suggest these conclusions: 1) there were rules within the community of faith from the earliest times, and some were memorialized in these founding documents; 2) the rules were formed or adopted in various ways and under particular historical circumstances; 3) the church changed and adapted its rules of conduct over time, even those once attributed to a divine source, "from the Lord."

Those who allege that there is no place for rules in a community of faith and love must deal with the clear evidence of these very early "regulations." But the earliest churches also possessed a sense of their own ability, under the guidance of the Spirit dwelling within them, to modify those rules to suit their needs and the changing times.

Each of the four instances—decision-making, conflict resolution, order in the assembly, and qualifications for leadership—focused on a ministry in action as well as on the rules for action which resulted. It is the ministry now described as canonical.

What's in a Name?

In one sense the argument of this book begins and ends with the meaning of the word *canon*. Canons are not the same as laws. Canon is a Greek word *(kanon)* meaning "rule." It did not and does not mean "law." Very early in the church's history this term, *kanon* (rule), was deliberately selected instead of the Greek word for law, *nomos*, or the Latin word for law, *lex*, to name the norms, decisions, or rules of behavior within the church. The church's canons were then and are today quite different from the *laws* of cities, states, and nations.

The etymology of the Greek word *kanon* and its Latin equivalent, *regula*, indicates its derivation from terms like "ruler," "yardstick," "measuring rod." That is, the term is derived from the instruments or standards that carpenters or stonemasons used to measure their work. *Canons* are rules or norms or measures of actions within the life of the church.

For many centuries the church's system of rules has been known by its Latin name *ius canonicum*, meaning "the canonical system," the norms proper to the church. It was used in contrast to *ius civile*, the civil system, norms proper to empires, kingdoms, and states.

The English expression "Canon Law" is both a redundancy and a misnomer. When it came time to translate *ius canonicum*, the church's system of rules, into English, the unfortunate choice was made to render *ius* by "law," which introduced the redundancy: literally "the canonical law" or "rule law." In other modern languages the Latin *ius* is translated by a word meaning a legal system, for example, *droit, diritto, derecho,* all of which convey the meaning of "the canonical system" when combined with *canonique, canonico,* (or *Kirchenrecht,* in German, "church law" or "the church's legal system").

The English term "Canon Law" not only trips over itself in its redundancy, but it gives the false impression that its rules are just like civil laws. They are not. As the rules of the churches, they are a system unique to the life of the churches.

For many centuries "canonical" has been understood to refer to the rules which regulate the life of Christian churches. That is the meaning which should endure, unencumbered by imagined parallels with civil legal systems.[4]

A LOOK BACK AT HISTORY

The church's system of rules *(kanones, ius canonicum)* is almost two thousand years old. Over that long period of time, the rules have served many different purposes. This is one reason why their basic identity is not always easy to discern. In part, their differing functions reflected the radically diverse roles which the church played in the larger society. The church, throughout its long history, has been many things in relation to its surrounding social and political contexts.

The church, the same communion which we identify with the Roman Catholic Church of today, has been:

- a small persecuted minority,
- the established church of the Roman Empire,
- an influential force in feudal society,
- a major power among the emergent nation-states in Europe,

- a controlling authority during the colonization of the "new worlds,"
- the governing regime over much of central Italy (the "papal states"), and, today,
- a worldwide *church* which has diplomatic relations with over one hundred *nations!*

The very diversity of the church's historic situations and mutations contributes to the current confusion about the nature and identity of Canon Law. It has been many things over a long period of time. Now the question arises again: What is Canon Law today? A few historical examples will serve to illustrate this ambiguous diversity.

The Christian Emperors

The Roman emperors Theodosius and Justinian compiled collections of the laws of the Roman Empire (the first in the year 438, the second in 534), enacted and enforced by their authority as emperors. Both collections contained large numbers of rules for the church and the church's ministers.

In other words, the church, even in the affairs internal to its communities and their sacramental lives, was regulated by norms *(constitutiones)* of the empire. Because it was the official church of the empire at that time, rules were made and enforced by imperial authority. Although the emperors were principally concerned with the relationship between religion and the public order, they did not hesitate to command disciplinary rules based on matters of religious doctrine, for example, that the sacrament of baptism could not be repeated, or that heretics could be punished.

Charlemagne

Charlemagne (742–814), the king of the Franks and Lombards who later became the Holy Roman Emperor, used Canon Law as a means of both renewing the church in central Europe and unifying his kingdom. He received a classic collection of canons, the Dionysian–Hadrian Collection, from the pope of Rome, Adrian I, in 774. He employed this book of the church's rules as a ready instrument for consolidating his imperial domain, most often through the process of local synods or councils of church reform.

Acting as Christian king and emperor, Charlemagne mainly circulated and enforced the church's own rules of life and good order. However, he also issued a number of edicts or decrees *(capitula)* for the church as Theodosius and Justinian had done before him, for example, rules on preaching and Sunday observance.

Papal Claims of Secular Power

Pope Gregory VII, in his struggle to free the church from its domination by secular rulers, in 1075 asserted the canonical authority not only to transfer or depose bishops, but to depose emperors as well.

Pope Boniface VIII claimed (in 1302 in the bull *Unam Sanctam*) that the power of kings was delegated to them by the papacy, and declared that "it is altogether necessary to salvation for every human creature to be subject to the Roman Pontiff."

In other words, for the sake of Christian liberty, the popes dared to claim that their canonical authority was superior to the "secular" power of kings and emperors, and that all authority was derived from theirs.

Authority of Concordats

The canonical rules established through the centuries by concordats present one more example of the anomalous nature of Canon Law. Concordats are the formal agreements between church and state, between ecclesiastical authority and civil power, more specifically in modern times, between the Apostolic See acting in the name of the church and national governments. Such bilateral church-state pacts have been employed scores of times since the eleventh century to resolve conflicts and provide for matters of mutual interest, for example, appointment of bishops, remuneration of clergy, freedom to operate schools.

The 1801 concordat between the Holy See and France under the rule of Napoleon is a case in point. The agreement gave public recognition to the Catholic Church in France, but it retained for the state the church's vast properties which had been confiscated after the Revolution. The concordat also reorganized all of the dioceses in France (reducing their number from 136 to 66), and gave the French government the right to present the candidates for bishops of the dioceses.

These church-state contracts produce juridic effects in both realms, canonical and civil, and their provisions prevail over the canons of the *Code of Canon Law* (confer canon 3 of the 1983 *Code*).

In Conclusion

In all four of these historic examples, the rules in question arc or were considered to be "canon law" *(ius canonicum)*. One would expect the rules for a religious community to originate and be enforced within that community. One would also expect the rules to oblige and regulate only its own members. These historical examples reveal something else.

Because of the church's diverse relationships with its surrounding societies, sometimes extremely cooperative, sometimes adversarial, its rules have originated in different ways and governed widely diverse matters. History hardly clarifies the nature of Canon Law. Quite the contrary, the radically diverse historical situations of the church have generated a cloud of ambiguity about what Canon Law really is.

This present time, after the church has come to terms with its most successful reform council, offers a unique opportunity to clarify the nature of the church's canonical system and canonical ministry. It is a new era, bright with possibility.

In the Second Vatican Council and in subsequent episcopal synods the church has looked long and deeply into its reflective mirror and discovered itself in new ways. The purpose, mission, and ministries of the church now stand out in sharper relief. The global, pluralistic, and ecumenical settings for the church reveal fresh and urgent needs. A ministry of Canon Law for a world church can now be described in a new way. And, although they may not know it now, the shape of this renewed ministry will make a difference to the people down at St. Mary's on Main Street.

CHAPTER 3

A VISION OF CHURCH:
THE THEOLOGICAL CONTEXT
FOR THE MINISTRY

THOSE ENGAGED IN CHURCH MINISTRY need a vision of the church and its mission to guide their work. The clearer and more accurate the vision, the more confident and effective will be the ministry. The purpose of this chapter is to sketch a theology of the church in order to provide a context for the ministry of canonists.

The canonical ministry, which is devoted to the freedom and good order of the church, demands an especially clear and accurate ecclesiological vision. Some other ministries, administration of property or personal counseling, for example, may be able to function effectively with a less profound or more ambiguous theology of church. Not so the ministry of Canon Law. An excellent theology of the church is a first priority.

The theological vision presented here, often termed "*communio* ecclesiology," is true to the New Testament data and to the teachings of the Second Vatican Council. It is an authentic and trustworthy ecclesiology. However, it is presented here as a sketch and does not purport to be a complete and fully detailed theology of church.[1]

33

The chapter sets forth the salient themes of the theology. It raises them up as points of emphasis in sufficient detail to reveal the outlines of a theological vision. These themes function like sight lines in a garden that focus one's view on a particular prospect. They lead to appealing views and provide a sense of the whole, but they do not reveal everything. There is much more of beauty and value to be explored.

The themes are: 1) local church as point of departure, 2) a community of word and sacrament, 3) enlivened and nourished by the Spirit, 4) existing in communion, 5) a part of the new people of God, 6) with a mission, 7) a member of the body of Christ, 8) a sacrament of salvation directed toward the future, 9) in continuity with the apostles, 10) yet one church, a single complex reality.

POINT OF DEPARTURE: LOCAL CHURCH

To be authentic and verifiable, a vision of the church must begin with the observable lived reality: the local congregations which *are* churches. The concrete, specific, and localized communities of believing people are the primary reality of the church, and this fact must never be lost from view. It is only by tenaciously holding these communities in the forefront, that an ecclesial vision can be accurate and reliable.

The "real weight" of local congregations keeps the theology of church anchored. Without it the notion of church tends to float skyward, adrift in generalized abstractions. Without the verifying element of local churches there is a terrible temptation to speculate about invisible internal structures, theoretical images, mental creations *(entia rationis),* and inflations of the mysterious.

Church exists, first and foremost, where human persons know one another and relate to one another, where they are initiated as Christ's disciples, where they gather to pray, where they cooperate in work and witness, and where they form a stable community.

St. Mary's on Main Street is church. What happens there on Sunday mornings and on weekday evenings is the life of the church. These particular people in their families and neighbor-hoods comprise this local church, and from their own ethnic and cultural backgrounds, with their own virtues and vices, strengths and weaknesses, they are the church.

What actually happens in the hundreds of thousands of stable, local Catholic congregations in all parts of the world is what makes up the church's vital activity. From small base communities to huge urban parishes, from very wealthy to extremely poor, from highly educated to completely illiterate—these diverse communities are churches, and it is their actual, living reality that must always be kept in view.

The Second Vatican Council taught:

> This church of Christ is truly present *(vere adest)* in all the legitimate local congregations of the faithful which, united to their shepherds, are themselves called churches in the New Testament. For in their own locality, these are the new people called by God in the Holy Spirit and with full conviction (cf. 1 Thes 1, 5). In these the faithful are gathered together by the preaching of the gospel of Christ and the mystery of Lord's supper is celebrated, "so that the whole fellowship is joined together through the flesh and blood of the Lord's body." In any community of the altar, under the sacred ministry of the bishop, there is made manifest the symbol of that charity and "unity of the mystical body without which there can be no salvation." In these communities, although frequently small and poor, or living far from one another, Christ is present by whose power the one, holy, catholic and apostolic church is gathered together. *(LG 26)*

The Catholic Church is made up of these local "altar communities," these myriad yet unique eucharistic congregations of the faithful. They are linked together in cities and regions to make up "particular churches" (called dioceses), which are in turn joined together in a worldwide union, the universal Roman Catholic Church.

The "universal church" exists only in the individual churches and is made up of them.[2] It is in the particular churches (dioceses) that "the one, holy, catholic and apostolic church of Christ is truly present and operative" (*CD* 11). The communion of these individual churches is the concrete form and realization of the one church universal.

Dioceses are not mere administrative units or subdivisions of the worldwide church. And the local churches, the parishes and other congregations which make up the dioceses, are not "branch offices" or "franchise outlets" of the diocese. In both instances, diocese and parish, they are complete embodiments of the church. The particular and the universal realizations of church dwell within one another, they are mutually inclusive.

The full reality of church exists in the local churches (parishes). All the essential elements of church are present in them: a human community, the call of God, the word of Christ, the presence and action of the Spirit, the celebration of the Eucharist, a fellowship of faith, hope, and love, and a connection to the ministry of the apostles. These constitutive principles generate and sustain a genuine church *(ekklesia).*

These local churches are not isolated or separate; they are always connected with the other communities of the diocese and the worldwide communion. But each one is not simply a part of the church, it is in itself fully church.

The church is not a huge general membership organization, like the American Association of Retired Persons with its thirty-three million dues-paying members, or like the Internet where millions of people simply obtain access and log on. Individuals become members of the church by baptism within a local congregation, not by enrollment at diocesan headquarters or by a spiritual connection with the bishop of Rome. Every active Catholic is affiliated with a local church. Persons belong to the universal church because they belong to a local community.

Local communities of the faithful, whether strong and thriving or weak and moribund, are the fundamental reality of the church. No theology of the church can prescind from or overlook this reality. It is both a point of departure and a constant point of reference.

Catholicism is irreducibly communal. It is made up of local communities. It is communitarian, not a vast composite of individual believers, nor some kind of massive collective. The Catholic Church is a communion of churches, a communion of local congregations.

COMMUNITIES OF WORD AND SACRAMENT

The twin forces of God's holy word and saving sacraments unite and empower local churches (*PO* 4, 5). Their communal life is nourished at the table of the Eucharist and the word of the gospel.[3] The active participation[4] of its members in these evangelical and sacramental events energizes their communities and gives voice to their praise of God. Word and sacrament for the churches are like sunshine and rainfall for living plants, dual sources of their life and growth.

God's revelation, embodied in the written word and in living tradition, is received by God's people in many ways. Believing people hear, read, study, discuss, and contemplate that life-giving word in various settings. However, they experience the word most powerfully and pervasively in its systematic proclamation and explanation in their local communities, most often within celebrations of the sacraments. Week in and week out, year after year, they listen to, reflect on, and respond to the word of God. Its truth and power forms them, their consciences, viewpoints, and understanding, and it shapes their communities. God's "story" is the story of the local church as it gradually transforms the believing community.

The local church becomes itself and expresses itself most intensely in its sacramental celebrations, especially in its celebrations of the Eucharist. The church is most fully and perfectly actualized when the people assemble and celebrate the memorial of the Lord's life, death, and rising. They gather around the table of the Lord to share in his life and in the lives of one another. The Eucharist is the peak achievement of the church as event. The gathered assembly, with presider and other ministers in its midst, is the acting subject together with the Risen Christ.

The church *enacts* itself in its eucharistic celebrations, with everyone playing a role: greeters, readers, ushers, singers, presider, communion givers, active participants all (*SC* 48). No one is to be there as stranger or mere spectator. However, it is healthy to recall that, as with any human activity, these celebrations are often flawed. At St. Mary's on Main Street sometimes the Sunday Masses fully express their reality, sometimes they fall short.

Liturgical celebrations in local churches are actions empowered by the Holy Spirit wherein Christ is present and God is worshiped. Because they are so central to the very nature of the church, manifestations of its true heart, the Council taught that "liturgy is the summit toward which the activity of the church is directed, and at the same time it is the fountain from which all its power flows" (*SC* 10).

While liturgy is central to the life of the local community, it must not be viewed as its entire life. In the covenanted life of the parish community, there is much more to its activity and witness than the hour or two of Sunday worship. Nevertheless, those liturgical moments of maximal activity and participation animate and focus the community for all its other activities.

Of all the church's communal actions, it is the Eucharist which expresses and affects the communion of the churches most emphatically. It builds and promotes the local congregation and explicitly connects it with all the other local churches throughout the diocese, nation, continent, and world.

THE ACTION OF THE HOLY SPIRIT

Christ is present in the celebration of the Eucharist through the power of the Holy Spirit and the instrumentality of the assembled faithful. The *epiclesis,* which is the petitionary prayer in the eucharistic canon, asks the Father to send the Spirit to make Christ present:

> Let your Spirit come upon these gifts to make them holy, so
> that they may become for us the body and blood of our Lord
> Jesus Christ. (Eucharistic Prayer II)

This prayer is a symbolic reminder of the powerful directive role
which the Spirit has in the entire life of the church. The church
quite literally *lives* by the Holy Spirit.

The central document of the Second Vatican Council,
Lumen Gentium, with strong reliance on the New Testament, put
it this way:

> When the work which the Father had given the Son to do on
> earth (Jn 17, 4) was accomplished, the Holy Spirit was sent
> on the day of Pentecost to sanctify the church continually so
> that all believers would have access to the Father through
> Christ in the one Spirit (Eph 2, 18). This is the Spirit of life,
> a fountain of water springing up for eternal life (Jn 4, 14; 7,
> 38–39), through whom the Father restores life to human
> beings who were dead through sin, until he raises up their
> mortal bodies in Christ (Rom 8, 10–11). The Spirit dwells in
> the church and in the hearts of the faithful as in a temple (1
> Cor 3, 16; 6, 19). He prays in them and bears witness to their
> adoption as children (Gal 4, 6; Rom 8, 15–16 and 26). The
> Spirit leads the church into all truth (Jn 16, 13), and makes it
> one in fellowship and ministry, instructing and directing it
> through a diversity of gifts, both hierarchical and charis-
> matic, and he adorns it with his fruits (Eph 4, 11–12; 1 Cor
> 12, 4; Gal 5, 22). Through the power of the gospel the Spirit
> makes the church grow, continually renews it, and leads it
> toward perfect union with its spouse. (*LG* 4)
>
> In order that we might be unceasingly renewed in him (Eph 4,
> 23), Christ has given us his Spirit, who is one and the same in
> head and members. This Spirit enlivens, unifies and moves
> the whole body, so that the fathers of the church could com-
> pare the Spirit's function to that which is exercised by the life-
> principle, the soul, in the human body. (*LG* 7)

In many other places the Council spoke strongly of the role
of the Spirit in the life of the church.[5] The Holy Spirit of God is

the impelling force and guiding light for the church in this world. The church is constituted and lives from the gifts of the Spirit. This enlivening indwelling of the Spirit is corporate as well as individual, that is, the Spirit dwells in and gives life to the gathered church *(ecclesia congregata)*, the community of the faithful, as well as to its individual members.

> It is the Holy Spirit, dwelling in those who believe and filling and ruling over the church as a whole, who brings about that wonderful communion of the faithful *(communio fidelium)*. He brings them all into intimate union with Christ, so that the Spirit is the principle of the church's unity. The distribution of graces and ministries is the Spirit's work too, enriching the church of Jesus Christ with different functions "in order to equip the saints for the work of service, so as to build up the body of Christ" (Eph 4, 12). (*UR* 2)

The Spirit's presence and power must be recognized and affirmed as central to any authentic vision of the church. However, the Western church has long neglected this pneumatological element in its ecclesiology, due in part to its historic conflicts with the Orthodox and Protestant Churches. As recently as the mid-twentieth century, Western theology acknowledged only two functions for the Spirit in relationship to the church: guaranteeing the teaching magisterium, and assisting the inner life of individual believers. The work of the Second Vatican Council went a long way toward correcting this centuries-old neglect of the Spirit.

The New Testament describes the extensive activities of the Holy Spirit related to the life of the church. The Spirit:

- gives life, empowers, energizes, renews;[6]
- teaches truth, bears witness, scrutinizes, instructs;[7]
- gives gifts, charisms, ministries;[8]
- prays, intercedes, advocates;[9]
- forgives, reconciles;[10]
- guides, leads, directs;[11]

- gathers, unifies, and builds up the community;[12]
- stands for freedom.[13]

These Spirit-actions are truly vital functions, like the circulation of blood and the breathing of air for the human body. They give life to the church and impel its mission, in local congregations, dioceses, and the worldwide communion.

The Holy Spirit dwells in the church as in a temple (Eph 2, 21–22), but not like a stone statue of a god standing in a Greek or Roman temple. The Spirit's presence is nourishing and invigorating, a life force that makes the small grove of the local church and the great forest of the universal church grow and flourish.

The Spirit gives gifts *(charismata)* to everyone, for benefit, for the common good. The Spirit distributes charisms, ministries, works, and energies freely and according to the Spirit's own initiative.[14] These talents or impulses are certainly not restricted to officeholders or hierarchs. They are widespread and recurrent, like wild flowers blooming everywhere. They are abundant even at St. Mary's on Main Street.

COMMUNION

The local church is the verification of any theology of church. And the powerful action of the Holy Spirit is a salient feature of that theology. However, it is the profound and multifaceted notion of "communion" *(koinonia)* which encompasses, orients, and coordinates all of ecclesiology.

The concept of "communion" is key to the comprehension of the nature of the church. It is a notion which lies at the very heart of the church's self-understanding. The word is derived from the Greek word used often in the New Testament: *koinonia,* meaning a sharing, a participation, a fellowship, a community. "The grace of the Lord Jesus Christ and the love of God and the fellowship *(koinonia)* of the Holy Spirit be with all of you" (2 Cor 13, 14) is a familiar greeting at eucharistic celebrations.

Meanings of Communion

Within the theology of the church the term "communion" applies or operates in many ways. It means:

Communion with God. This describes the sharing by all humankind, and in a special way by baptized Christian believers, in the life of the Triune God. Communion implies the presence of grace, the indwelling of the Holy Spirit.

Communion of the faithful. The *communio fidelium* speaks of the active and coresponsible participation of each member of the church in its life, its faith, and its worship. The "common priesthood" and the sharing of all believers in the prophetic office *(sensus fidelium)* are functions of this use of communion (*LG* 10 and 12).

Communion of the saints. The *communio sanctorum* links Christians across space and time. It joins together those in all regions of the earth as well as those who have gone before and those yet to be born.

Communio sanctorum. The same Latin expression also carries the sense of "partaking of holy things," that is, the sharing in word and sacrament. It conveys a belief in and commitment to the gospel of Jesus Christ and in those liturgical actions which celebrate his life, death, and rising.

Holy Communion. Eucharistic sharing means partaking of the bread and wine which is the body and blood of Christ at the table of the Lord. This sacramental contact with the very person of Christ and with our fellow communicants is the paramount sign of full incorporation in the church.

Communion of the churches. The *communio ecclesiarum* is the bond among the local churches which make up a diocese as well as that among the particular churches which constitute the church universal. It defines the Catholic Church.

Ecumenical communion. In another sense *communio ecclesiarum* represents the Great Church, the Christian reality which is larger and wider than that church which subsists in the Roman Catholic Church. It is the manifold and strong, but partial, communion which links the Christian churches to one another by many common bonds.

Hierarchical communion. Communio hierarchica stands for the sacramental and juridical communion among bishops, presbyters, and deacons. It is an expression of the unity of the episcopal college together with its head, the successor of Peter; of the presbyteral college together with its head, the diocesan bishop; and of the order of deacons with its bishop and presbyterate.

Human communion. This stands for the multifold communality which links all of humankind. It undergirds the fundamental unity, solidarity, and interdependence of all sisters and brothers on earth, all of whom are the concern of the church.

Communion of all living things. This is a reminder of all the physical and moral connections, grounded in creation, redemption, and common destiny, within the one cosmos which humans share with all other living creatures and with the environment.

In sum, *communio,* a most flexible and polysemous concept, expresses the very warp and woof of the church, its vital activity, its unity and catholicity. The venerable notion of *communio* is "not some vague *disposition,* but *an organic reality* which requires juridic form and at the same time is animated by charity."[15] It is a central and controlling concept in ecclesiology.

Aspects of Communion Pertinent to This Ecclesiology

The deepest meaning of "communion" is the participation of the human person in the very life of God: "our fellowship *(koinonia)* is with the Father and with his Son Jesus Christ" (1 Jn 1, 3); "you were called to fellowship with his Son, Jesus Christ our Lord" (1 Cor 1, 9). Fellowship with God is the fundamental meaning of communion. Each of the divine Persons had a role in fashioning this participation (*LG* 2–4), but the Holy Spirit uniquely dwells in, gives life to, guides and directs, grows and renews the communion called church (*LG* 4). St. Augustine taught that communion is the work proper *(opus proprium)* to the Holy Spirit.

This profound and precious gift of "communion" with God, through God's own free initiative, grounds another, closely related meaning of communion, namely that intimate bond between those called by God to be his children. Communion joins together all those baptized into Christ, and it joins together the communities into which they were baptized. "This messianic people...has been set up by Christ as a communion of life, love and truth" (*LG* 9). The Holy Spirit enlivens both the believing individuals and the congregations into which they are gathered as church.[16]

The earliest Christians were conscious of their close connections with one another, for example, "they devoted themselves to the teaching of the apostles and to the communal life."[17] They were likewise aware of sharing in the Spirit, that is, "the participation in the Holy Spirit."[18] They took care of one another, for example, "All who believed were together and had all things in common" (Acts 2, 44), and they looked after the needs of the other communities. This was exemplified in the concern of the church in Jerusalem for the divisions within the church at Antioch (Acts 15), and the contributions of the churches in Macedonia, Achaia, and Corinth to the impoverished community in Jerusalem.[19] Thus "communion" expresses most aptly and authentically the graced and animated unity of the church.

The sharing described as "holy communion," partaking in the Lord's Supper, symbolizes and strengthens all three forms of participation: in the life of God, among the communities, and within the churches.

> The cup of blessing that we bless, is it not a participation *(koinonia)* in the blood of Christ? The bread that we break, is it not a participation in the body of Christ? Because the loaf of bread is one, we, though many, are one body, for we all partake of the one loaf. (1 Cor 10, 16–17)

Christians' participation in the Risen Lord present in the Eucharist grounds and fosters their unity with one another. That is to say, the church is built up by the celebration of the Eucharist.[20] "When we really participate in the body of the Lord through the breaking of the eucharistic bread, we are raised up to communion with him and among ourselves" (*LG* 7).

Eucharistic communion is the climactic expression of the church's vitality and unity, its expressive summit, and it is built upon the larger communion of word and sacrament. The entirety of God's holy word and all sacramental celebrations build up and show forth the communion of the church's life (*LG* 11).

In addition to their sharing at the Lord's tables of word and sacrament, early Christians manifested their "communion" with each other and among the local churches in many other tangible ways. They sent charitable assistance[21] to poorer churches, they prayed for other churches by name at their liturgies, and they sent consecrated bread to other communities. Neighboring bishops gathered to lay hands on the newly chosen leader of a local church. Representatives of the churches in a region came together in synods or councils. Letters (*litterae pacis*) were sent from one church to another asking for hospitality or safe conduct, or granting reconciliation to penitents. Churches, especially in the West, gradually acknowledged the influence of the church of Rome in certain matters. All of these activities testified vividly to the mutual recognition and acceptance which showed the very real "communion" which existed among the churches.

The sense of communion which existed among local churches was demonstrated also by its denial or removal. A local church, together with its bishop, was sometimes refused communion (eucharistic and otherwise) because of a serious doctrinal errors (e.g., heresy), moral failure (e.g., simony), or disciplinary irregularity (e.g., rebaptism of apostates). The restoration of full communion, that cherished sense of solidarity and belonging, when withdrawn by other churches, was eagerly sought by the offending community. This keen sense of communion, among individual members of the faithful as well as among the local churches in which they gathered, has endured in Catholic tradition through the centuries.

The communion of the churches *(communio ecclesiarum)* which *is* the church universal was firmly taught by the Second Vatican Council: the one unique catholic church exists in and from the particular churches.[22] In other words, the worldwide church only exists in the particular churches and is built up out of them.

The same reality is reflected within the particular churches (dioceses): they exist in and from the local churches, that is, in and from parishes and other local congregations within their boundaries. The diocese, as church, exists only in local churches, like St. Mary's on Main Street, and is built up out of them. The diocese is a communion of local churches in the same way that the universal church is a communion of dioceses.

The collegiate structures of the worldwide episcopate and of the diocesan presbyterate *(communio hierarchica)* are parallel to and representative of this communion of churches.[23] The churches are the prior reality, then the apostolic, ministerial leadership within them. The leaders change, the churches endure. But in both instances, diocesan and universal, the ministerial leaders manifest the communion of churches and project the solidarity and solicitude which those churches are obliged to show for one another because of the churches' communion with each another.

The Elements of Communion

The ecclesial reality of communion is made up of many different elements, like the varicolored strands of a woven belt. Some of these components were enunciated by the Second Vatican Council as the factors required for full incorporation in the church.

These are:

- possession of the Spirit of Christ,
- acceptance of the church's whole order *(integram ordinationem)* and all of the means of salvation established within it,
- union with Christ within the church's visible framework (which Christ rules through the pope and the bishops) by

means of the bonds of the profession of faith, the sacraments, ecclesiastical governance, and communion,
- perseverance in charity, and response to Christ's grace in thought, word, and deed.[24]

The Council also described other elements of communion when it spoke of the connections between the Catholic Church and other Christians. These are:

- acceptance of sacred scripture as normative, sincere religious zeal, belief in God the Father and Christ as savior,
- baptism in Christ, acceptance of other sacraments,
- the episcopate, celebration of the Eucharist, devotion to Mary,
- prayers and other spiritual benefits,
- the bond of the Holy Spirit, from whom comes sanctifying gifts and graces, strengthening some even to martyrdom.[25]

The Council went on to detail further the elements and endowments by which Christians are joined in communion, albeit imperfectly. These are:

- justification by faith in baptism, and incorporation into Christ,
- the written word of God, the life of grace, faith, hope, and charity, and other interior gifts of the Holy Spirit,
- visible elements, and the celebration of sacred actions of the Christian religion.

The life of grace engendered by these elements gives access to the "communion of salvation" (communio salutis).[26]

In sum, the elements or the "content" of communion is complex and manifold. The precise elements have been differently described depending on the context, that is, whether referring to the communion between believing persons, between local churches, or between Christian denominations.

THE PEOPLE OF GOD

The revival of the concept of the "people of God" to describe the church was one of the crowning achievements of the Second Vatican Council (*LG* 9–17). The notion deepens the realization of the church as *communio,* locates the church within the history of salvation, links it to the chosen people of Israel, and identifies those called by God who respond to the message of Christ.

> This messianic people has Christ for its head....This people has been given the dignity and the freedom of sons and daughters of God, in whose hearts the Holy Spirit dwells as in a temple. For its law it has the new commandment of love...and for its goal it has the kingdom of God....It constitutes for the whole human race a most solid seed of unity, hope and salvation. It was set up by Christ as a communion of life, love and truth...and sent to the whole world as the light of the world and the salt of the earth. (*LG* 9)

The concept of the people of God transcends the laity-hierarchy dualism, and points to the communality and solidarity of a single people. It depicts a people on the march through history, a pilgrim people, but a people united and empowered. Within this one people there are functions, ministries, charisms, and religious vocations, but no special status or separate classes. Their common existence as a people precedes and underlies all distinctions based on office or ministry or gift.

The people of the "new covenant"[27] all share in the three-fold ministry and mission of Christ (*LG* 10–13). All of the baptized are consecrated as a holy priesthood, they all share in Christ's prophetic mission, and everyone assists in gathering humankind into this "new and universal people of the children of God":

> For this finally God sent the Spirit of his Son, the Lord and giver of life, who is for the church and for each and every one of the faithful the principle of union and of unity in the

teaching of the apostles, in communion, in the breaking of bread and in prayers.[28]

Those who belong to this people, enlivened and encouraged by the Spirit of Christ, are full and active participants in its life and works.

The "people of God" is not an undifferentiated mass of human beings. Rather there are many shades of diversity within this unity. This one people is made up of distinct groups. The groups differ in geography, history, race, and culture as well as in spiritual and liturgical traditions. "By virtue of this catholicity, the individual parts bring their own gifts to the other parts and to the whole church" (*LG* 13). These parts of the church, including individuals and local churches, are bound together in one intimate communion. They are all members of the people of God, linked by various bonds, including that of mutual assistance.

The notion of belonging to a "people" underscores the humanness of the church. It leads to the expectation of weakness, waywardness, mistakes, and sins. These human failings have been part and parcel of the church's life since the outset, for example, the dishonesty of Ananias and Saphira (Acts 5, 1–11), conflicts between the Greek-speaking and Hebrew-speaking disciples in Jerusalem (Acts 6), incest and drunkenness (1 Cor 5 and 11).

The people of God, of course, is much larger than the Catholic Church. All human persons are called to belong, all are ordered to it in some way, and all of those who believe in Christ belong. The Catholic Church is properly described as one part of this people.

Full, conscious, and active participation in the life of the church, and not only in its liturgical celebrations, is the right and duty of the Christian faithful, "the chosen race, the royal priesthood, the holy nation, the people of whom God has taken possession."[29] At St. Mary's on Main Street this level of full and active sharing on the part of all is an ideal not often achieved. However, it is the rightful expectation of God's people, and hence it always remains the goal of pastoral activity there and in all local churches.

The lay members of the Christian faithful actually perform most of the teaching, sanctifying, and ruling within this people of God, even though those functions *(munera)* are associated with the ordained. Consider the teaching about God which parents, catechists, and religion teachers do in local churches. Consider the formation of moral character which goes on in homes and schools and workplaces. Consider the convening, organizing, and coordinating of all manner of activities which take place in every parish. The lay members of God's people do the overwhelming majority of this work.

To draw attention to those who actually do the majority of the work in these central areas of church life is not to overlook the irreplaceable energy of God's Spirit, nor to diminish the enormous efforts and guidance of ordained ministers. It simply points to the real levels of active participation in the life of this people of God called church.

MISSION

There is some danger that a vision of the church which begins with the local congregation and its sacramental life, and which focuses on the multivalent communion of the people of God, might appear to be turned inward on itself. A community preoccupied with itself and concerned mainly about its own health and well-being would be a tragic distortion of the true vision of church.

"The pilgrim church is missionary by its very nature" (*AG* 2). To be missionary means to be sent. The church takes its origin from the sending of the Son and the Holy Spirit by God the Father, and the sending of the disciples by Jesus. The church exists to carry out those missions and not simply to perpetuate itself.

The saving work of Christ is the church's central task. It performs that task by making itself fully present to all peoples and nations, so that by the example of its life and preaching it might lead them to the faith, the freedom, and the peace of Christ (*AG* 5). Christ was sent to preach the gospel to the poor:

> The Spirit of the Lord is upon me, because he has anointed me to bring glad tidings to the poor. He has sent me to proclaim liberty to captives and recovery of sight to the blind, to let the oppressed go free, and to proclaim a year acceptable to the Lord. (Lk 4, 18–19)

> The church, urged on by the Spirit of Christ, ought to go the same road that Christ went, namely a road of poverty, obedience, service and self-sacrifice even unto death. (*AG* 5)

The church is oriented outward. Its activities are not limited to its own community, nor circumscribed by its own interests. The local church raises its sights and looks beyond itself. It reaches out for evangelization, but also for witness and work in the world around it. The believing community extends itself in assistance and cooperation to the other communities which surround it, as well as those farther afield.

> The church...proceeds on its way together with the whole of humanity and shares the world's earthly lot....The church pursues its saving purpose...in healing and ennobling the dignity of the human person, strengthening the fabric of human society, and investing the daily activity of men and women with a deeper meaning and importance. (*GS* 40)

The church's purpose is a religious one, but it can assist in the building and strengthening of the human community. At times it can and should initiate works to serve everyone, especially the needy. The church recognizes the good in contemporary social movements, especially developments toward unity. It respects and fosters whatever is true, good, and just in human institutions (*GS* 42).

Action on behalf of justice and participation in the transformation of the world is a constitutive dimension of the preaching of the gospel or, in other words, of the church's mission for the redemption of the human race and its liberation from every oppressive situation.[30]

St. Mary's on Main Street demonstrates its sense of mission in several ways: its connections with the Parroquia de San Miguel in rural Guatemala and with St. Martin de Porres parish across town, its support of a soup kitchen in the church basement, its home visitors project, and its active engagement in the urban renewal effort in its own neighborhood.

THE BODY OF CHRIST

The metaphor of a body for a multitude of persons points to their connectedness and mutual interdependence. The image also serves to emphasize the life and spirit which the people have in common.

Paul repeatedly compared the church and its members to the human body and its various parts:

> For as in one body we have many parts, and all the parts do not have the same function, so we, though many, are one body in Christ and individually parts of one another. (Rom 12, 4)

> As a body is one though it has many parts, and all the parts of the body, though many, are one body, so also Christ.... Now you are Christ's body, and individually parts of it.[31]

The hand is not the foot, the eye is not the ear; however, each one of the body parts depends on the others. If one part is hurt, all feel the pain. "If one part is honored, all the parts share its joy" (1 Cor 12, 26). The central message of the metaphor is that each person is differently gifted, and although those different abilities need to be acknowledged, each must collaborate in the common task.

The body of Christ is a strong symbol for the cohesion and participation of all of the members of the local church. Paul repeatedly used the body metaphor when addressing local churches and the ministries exercised within them.

Paul called Christ the head of the body,[32] thus calling attention not only to the common life which Christians share with him and because of him, but also to the authority and direction which the church has from Christ.

It is by the communication of the Holy Spirit that individuals are made brothers and sisters of Christ in the one body. "For by one Spirit we are all baptized into one body" (1 Cor 12, 13). When sharing in the body of the Lord through the breaking of the eucharistic bread, we are raised up to communion with him and among ourselves. The one Spirit distributes his various gifts for the good of the church according to his own riches and the needs of the ministries. "The same Spirit makes the body one by his power and by the inner cohesion of the members, and he urges and produces charity among the faithful" (*LG* 7). This Spirit, who is one and the same in head and members, gives life and movement to the body, and so can be compared to its soul.

The church, even though rightly called the body of Christ, is in pilgrimage on this earth, and subject to tribulation and persecution. Indeed, the truly human state of the church, like the true humanity of Jesus, must never be lost from our sight. With it come all the vicissitudes, travails, and disappointments of the human condition.

St. Mary's on Main Street is one of those communities of grace in which personal relations are not always easy and projects not always successful. Opinions differ, conflicts occur, factions exist. Like most other parishes, it is well aware of its humanity.

A SACRAMENT OF SALVATION

The Council, in the opening paragraph of its most solemn teaching about the nature and mission of the church, affirmed that the church is like "a sacrament or sign and instrument of intimate union with God and of the unity of all humanity" (*LG* 1). Later in the same document, the Council said it again:

> Christ, when he was lifted up from the earth, drew all people to himself; rising from the dead, he sent his lifegiving Spirit down on his disciples and through that Spirit he constituted his body which is the church as the universal sacrament of salvation. (*LG* 48)

In its final document, the Council stated the same truth even more forcefully:

> Whatever good God's people can contribute to the human family, in the period of its earthly pilgrimage, derives from the church's being "the universal sacrament of salvation," which shows forth and at the same time brings into effect the mystery of God's love for humanity.[33]

This teaching is truly astonishing: the church itself is a sacrament,[34] that is, the community of believers both reveals and furthers God's plan of salvation.[35] Humanity is able to discern in the church an active manifestation of the Christian plan of salvation. The saving events of Christ's life, death, and resurrection, in which the love of God was made visible and tangible on earth, are revealed in the life and witness of the church. Most significantly the church also "announces and inaugurates" the fulfillment of the mystery of "the kingdom of Christ and of God" of which it is the "seed and beginning" on earth (*LG* 5).

This amazing claim is brought within the bounds of human reality by the acknowledgment that the church is "at one and the same time holy and always in need of purification."[36] It is a church of sinners, and must continually seek repentance and renewal. The church, since it is fully human, is always cast in shadow, partially obscured by ordinary foible and failure.

This "sacrament of God's salvation" is embodied in a pilgrim people fully enmeshed in the world and the world's history. As such, the church is both enriched and burdened by its own history and endowed with an eschatological dynamism. It is, as it were, "pushed" by its own past, but also "pulled" into the future which is its destiny. God's people has the kingdom as its goal (*LG* 9). The church is eschatologically oriented, it is drawn forward in hope and expectation toward the final fulfillment of all things.

The Vatican Council spoke forcefully of the "eschatological character of the pilgrim church":

The church...will reach its completion only in the glory of heaven, when the time for the restoration of all things will come....

Christ...sent his lifegiving Spirit down on his disciples and through the Spirit he constituted his body which is the church as the universal sacrament of salvation....The promised restoration, therefore, which we await, has already begun in Christ, is advanced through the mission of the Holy Spirit and by means of the Spirit continues in the church in which, through faith, we are instructed about the meaning of our temporal life, while we...bring to its conclusion the work entrusted to us in the world by the Father....

However, until the arrival of the new heavens and the new earth,...the pilgrim church in its sacraments and institutions, which belong to this age, takes on the appearance of this passing world. (*LG* 48)

Again, when reflecting on the church's own task in today's world, the Council taught:

The church was initiated by the love of the eternal Father, was founded in history by Christ the redeemer and was made one by the Holy Spirit, and it has a saving and eschatological function which can be fully discharged only in the age to come. Yet it is now present on earth, composed of people who are members of the earthly city and are summoned to constitute, even now in human history, the family of God's children....Thus the church, as at the same time "an identifiable group and a spiritual community," proceeds on its way with the whole of humanity and shares the world's earthly lot, while being a leaven and, as it were, a soul of human society, which is to be renewed in Christ and transformed into God's family. (*GS* 40)

From this future-oriented aspect of the church as a sacrament of salvation, its eschatological dimension, at least three things follow:

1) the church's own provisional nature, always unfinished, always imperfect, a work in progress;

2) the church's commitment to the human project, its inextricable engagement in the human struggle, its lot is cast with humankind, especially the poor and suffering;

3) the church's abiding confidence, based on its hope in the Risen Christ and in the Holy Spirit, the guarantee of our inheritance (Eph 1, 14), that God's design for the world will ultimately be achieved.

Like the anticipation, seeding, and caring that goes into planning and planting a garden, which is always changing and never fully realized, so the pilgrim people lives with a hope-filled longing for a fulfillment yet to come.

The church, in particular the local church, always *strives* to be a sacrament of salvation, to show forth the mystery of God's love for humanity. The congregations of the faithful must challenge themselves to be efficacious signs of God's saving grace within their own neighborhoods, towns, and cities. Christian communities, like all individual believers, are also called to continual repentance and conversion. They must seek to rise above their introversion and self-absorption and to extend generous hands to other communities, just as the earliest Christian churches did.[37]

Can local churches, through the quality of their life in communion and by their actions on behalf of their neighbors, provide a pattern for those who long for meaning, for community, for justice, and for peace?[38] St. Mary's, though flawed, strives to be a sacrament, a sign, and an instrument of unity, peace, and freedom for others on Main Street. Sometimes this is obvious to others, more often it occurs in ways that are small and obscure.

APOSTOLIC

Apostolicity is one of the ways that Christian communities measure their authenticity. "Apostolic," in conformity with the apostles, means that the community is aware of carrying on the message and memory of Jesus who was the messenger of God's salvation for humankind. Jesus summoned and sent forth a band of disciples whom he also called apostles (Mk 3, 13–19). After Jesus departed from this earth, each local congregation of his followers was then and is today conscious of being "the household of God, built upon the foundations of the apostles and prophets, with Christ Jesus himself as the capstone" (Eph 2, 19–20).

The church looks forward as well as back; it lives from the remembrance of Jesus Christ, but also in expectation of his return. Apostolicity is the assurance of continuity in the meantime. It means that there will be substantial identity in the Christian way of life until the Lord comes again.

Apostolicity is both a gift and a task. It implies God's reliable assistance ("I am with you always" Mt 28, 20)...as well as a constant challenge for the church on its mission, the challenge to remain faithful. The Holy Spirit is the ultimate source of this identity and fidelity. The Spirit empowered the apostles and disciples to bear witness to Jesus, that is, to recall and affirm what he had done and to anticipate his return:

> You will receive power when the Holy Spirit comes upon you, and you will be my witnesses...to the ends of the earth. (Acts 1, 8)

> We are witnesses of these things, as is the Holy Spirit that God has given to those who obey him. (Acts 5, 32)

> When the Advocate comes whom I will send you from the Father, the Spirit of truth that proceeds from the Father, he will testify to me. And you also testify, because you have been with me from the beginning. (Jn 15, 26)

The early communities were conscious of the powerful presence of the Spirit guiding and directing their efforts. In the Acts of the Apostles and in the epistles the authors speak of being sent, appointed, circumvented, led, and bound by the Spirit. Their preaching was through the Holy Spirit (1 Pt 1, 12), their decisions were made with the Spirit (Acts 15, 28), the church was built up with the help of the Spirit (Acts 9, 31), and their apostolic ministry was of the Spirit (2 Cor 3, 4–18). To lie to the apostles was to lie to the Holy Spirit (Acts 5, 3 and 9). Timothy was told to guard the rich heritage of testimony which had been entrusted to him "with the help of the Holy Spirit that dwells within us" (2 Tm 1, 14).

Apostolicity as gift is given by the Spirit to the community of believers first of all. Apostolicity as task is primarily a work of the *entire body of the faithful,* assisted by the Spirit. It is the *church* that is apostolic, and the Spirit that makes it apostolic. The Spirit came upon the assembled church at Pentecost (Acts 2, 1). The apostolicity of the church is a communion with the apostles, and through them with the Father and the Son (1 Jn 1, 1–3).

The church, flawed and errant as it sometimes has been (*GS* 43), is ultimately indefectible, because of the Spirit's gift and guidance.

> The holy people of God has a share, too, in the prophetic role of Christ, when it renders him a living witness....The universal body of the faithful who have received the anointing of the holy one, cannot be mistaken in belief. (*LG* 12)

The bishops' place in succession to the "traditioning" role of the apostles is a ministry to the community, not a personal prerogative. It must always be viewed within the apostolicity of the whole church, and never apart from or over against it.[39]

Apostolic succession means continuity in faith, in witness, in service, and in suffering. The central focus of this apostolicity is the "gospel," the good news of the life and death, the teaching and wondrous works of Jesus of Nazareth. This kernel of the Christian message is called the "entrusted pledge"[40] or the sound "teaching."[41] The New Testament bears witness to the faith and practices of the earliest Christian communities, and this remains the first measure of the faith and practices of today's local churches.

This New Testament message has priority. It is the unbroken continuity of teaching in the apostolic tradition. Each particular ministry at every moment in history is subject to this word from God. Those who assist the community in the transmission of the gospel are subordinate to that gospel.

> This teaching function is not above the word of God, but stands at its service, teaching nothing but what is handed down, according as it devotedly listens, reverently preserves and faithfully transmits the word of God, by divine command and with the help of the holy Spirit. (*DV* 10)

The Spirit's gift[42] is present in all local congregations. Local churches, like St. Mary's on Main Street, cannot make the same claim to indefectibility which is promised to the universal body of the faithful, but they have the same obligation to nurture the apostolicity of the local church within the apostolic tradition, and to persist as authentic "communities of Jesus."

ONE CHURCH: A SINGLE COMPLEX REALITY

A final theme within this theological vision of the church discloses its unique unity:

> Christ...established his holy church here on earth as a visible structure, a community of faith, hope and love, and he sustains it unceasingly....This society, however, equipped with hierarchical structures, and the mystical body of Christ, a visible assembly and a spiritual community, an earthly church and a church enriched with heavenly gifts, must not be considered as two things, but as forming one complex reality comprising a human and a divine element. (*LG* 8)

There are not two churches, but one. It is not one church supernatural, invisible and perfect, and another church human, visible, and sinful, but *one church*. The church is one, a single complex reality.

The Council dared to speak of the incarnate Word as an analogy for the church. Jesus Christ is one person, not a man with God lurking behind or hovering over him. The divine word assumed human nature, inseparably, as a living instrument of salvation. "In a similar way the social structure of the church serves the Spirit of Christ" (*LG* 8).

The analogy must be used with great care, since the hypostatic union in Jesus Christ is unique, an unparalleled union with God which implied sinlessness and fullness of truth. There is no hypostatic union between the Holy Spirit and the church, but the Spirit does make use of the visible structures and ministries of the church, as flawed and fallible as they are, as instruments of salvation.

The point is that the church is one entity. The visible human communities, the local assemblies of believers *are* that church. They are not a facade or screen for some other, more hidden, mystical reality. It is St. Mary's on Main Street, a people, congregation and ministers, that *is* the church, gifted by and in service to the Holy Spirit of God. It is one reality.

In Conclusion

This multifaceted vision of the church, proffered here as an authentic theology of church to guide canonical ministry, concludes with this metaphor.

A great forest is like the church, and the local churches are the trees within it. The forest is made up of many thousands of trees. Some are young, some are ancient. Some are strong and flourishing, some weak, endangered, dying. They all draw upon the moisture and nutrients in the soil. They share the air and sunlight and rain which make them grow. Each tree has its own identity and vitality; each lives its own life, each one can thrive or be cut down. But every tree is related to those around it. They depend on one another for germination, protection, and nourishment. The thousands of trees, each one with its own beauty and distinctiveness, make up one forest and the forest does not exist without the trees.

CHAPTER 4

CHURCHES IN PLACE:

THE SITUATIONAL CONTEXT

FOR THE MINISTRY

LOCAL AND PARTICULAR CHURCHES, parishes and dioceses, are always in the foreground for the canonical minister. Parishes and other local Catholic congregations are the primary manifestations of church, and dioceses are groupings of parishes, those portions of the people of God entrusted to a bishop. In the diocese the local churches are gathered together and united by the bishop in the Holy Spirit through the gospel and the Eucharist. These two realizations of church have the first claim on the professional ministry of the canonist. In order to serve them well the canonists must be guided by good theology and possess a vivid sense of the *place* of each church.

The local situation of every parish community is one of its constitutive elements. That is to say, the demographic and geographic particularity of each local church is not merely the setting or stage on which its life and activities are played out. Rather, the human specificity of each local church is an integral part of its very nature. It is far more than an element of a church's description.

The local church is a human manifestation of God's action in the world, and the church's human community, in all its specificity and particularity, is an instrument, an "embodiment," of the Holy Spirit (*LG* 7). Although the Holy Spirit's active and powerful presence in each church community is not the same as the Son's hypostatic union with the human nature of Jesus, it is analogous, and the actual human situation of each particular and parochial church commands the same serious theological consideration that the humanity of Christ does.

"Church" is not an idealized and abstract reality. Churches are stable communities of Christian women, men, and children in concrete places and specific times. Each has a history and a future, and its own particular circumstances. Each community thrives or suffers in a political and economic setting, each claims and clings to its own ethnic and cultural identity. Each Catholic congregation, like each individual human person, is unique. There is no such thing as "generic church." The uniqueness of each congregation demands recognition and attention.

This is not to suggest that each local church and its ministry is isolated or aloofly independent. Quite the contrary, each possesses within it the fullness of catholicity, each embodies the church universal, and each church is tied in close communion with all the others; it fails as church if it sunders communion. However, the community and its ministers must be sensitive to its particular situation, that is, to its unique locale and human texture. The ministers must address and respond to the needs of this specific congregation in the here and now.

These "particularities of place" or local differences make up the cultural identity of local churches. Each congregation is defined by a set of human realities which include these factors: 1) linguistic, 2) ethnic, 3) political, 4) economic, 5) religious, 6) geographic, 7) historic, 8) educational, 9) employment.

This chapter concludes with a reminder about two key principles of Catholic social teaching which relate to local churches, namely 1) subsidiarity, and 2) solidarity.

PARTICULARITIES OF PLACE: ELEMENTS

Language

Language shapes and colors the thinking of every people, it both reflects and molds their very identity. Language—French, Spanish, German, Mandarin, English—affects far more than names and messages, it forms and shades the perceptions, understandings, and the very lives of the people. It is part of the warp and woof of all culture.

The subtle influences and import of language are greater in matters of family or religion than in less personal affairs, like travel, commerce, or technology. People cherish their own familiar language for private prayer, for public worship, for commemorating life's great events: birth and baptism, weddings and anniversaries, deaths and funerals.

The battles which have been fought over vernacular translations of liturgical language since the Second Vatican Council bear witness to the centrality and sensitivity of language in worship and in other faith expressions. These conflicts have raised passions and caused divisions in local parishes, in religious communities, and in bishops' conferences. On the other hand, language is a strong unitive force in local churches as well; sometimes it is the bond which holds the members together as a community.

Ministry requires a constant sensitivity to language as an issue. The ministry of the canonist must include a knowledge of the language of the people and the cultural issues related to or expressed in that language. It implies inviting participation and consultation in the language and mode of the people, making announcements, decisions, and rules available in their style and idiom, rather than in awkward translations from Latin. It calls for the ability to find apt vernacular expression for the nuances of religious language and church practice.

At St. Mary's on Main Street, one Mass each weekend is celebrated in Spanish, but the Hispanic members of the parish still find it difficult to participate in other parish activities.

Ethnicity and Race

Ethnicity is like a lens through which all of life is viewed, a filter which shades the way that everything is received. Racial and ethnic background conditions peoples' perceptions and reactions to all of life's events, whether joyful, tragic, or just routine. It influences emotional responses, attitudes toward others, family practices, customary observances, choices of food, even manner of dress and ways of gesturing or walking.

Some ethnic patterns can remain the same for generations, even centuries. "This is the way we have always done it; it's the way we are." On the other hand, some ethnically rooted features change when set in a new context or are eroded as a people is placed in contact with another ethnic group.

Immigrants initially cling to their traditional ways as vital for their survival and identity. They find them changed, almost inevitably, within a generation or two. Ethnics may not "homogenize" or "melt" when transported and intermingled, but their characteristics do change over time, as a people is assimilated into the dominant culture, and they often change radically.

Today's global communications—radio, movies, records, tapes, the Internet, and especially television—influence and modify nearly all ethnic groups in the world. Ethnic factors emerge and strongly influence the expression of religious matters. Songs, movements, postures, and popular piety vary greatly. Attitudes toward the sacred, toward ordained ministers, toward the community are ethnically distinctive.

Polish immigrants to North America came with different expectations of their churches and pastors than did the Irish, the Germans, or the Italians. The Dutch and French missionaries affected the religious sense of African Christians in very different ways. Many ethnically based factors impinge on local churches like St. Mary's on Main Street, sometimes subtly, sometimes stridently. The "Hispanic Mass" on Sundays is only the most obvious one.

The ministry of the canonist needs to be fully informed about the ethnic nature of the community being served, especially if that ethnic background is mixed or different from the canonist's own. The minister should know and appreciate the values and traits of the ethnic groups. What are the patterns of their religious practice? How is the church and its authority viewed in this ethnic tradition? What is their sense of sacramental life? Are the people accustomed to support the church? What devotions and saints are important to them? What are their marriage and family values and practices? Depending on these circumstances, the canonist may need to encourage or support some pastoral accommodations.

Political Systems

Political ideas and systems can pervade people's attitudes toward authority and influence their values. Strong monarchies and dictatorships set up a certain set of expectations and reactions, while egalitarian democracies tend to encourage others. Both can profoundly affect thinking within the local churches as well as among church leaders. Acceptance of monarchical or of democratic forms of government in the secular sphere engenders expectations of a similar exercise of authority in the church. These political frames of reference, when internalized and deeply ingrained, can have effects on a people's sense of legitimate authority, rights of participation, justice and fairness, autonomy, and personal responsibility.

Both radically egalitarian societies and those with tightly guarded systems of rank, caste, and privilege powerfully influence life within the church community. In the cases of feudalism in western Europe, slavery in the United States, or apartheid in South Africa, the system led the powerful to expect to be treated with deference within their faith community as well as in society. This is in contrast to the deprived or disadvantaged class (serfs, slaves, nonwhites) who often tolerated a "second-class citizenship" within their churches, when in fact they were entitled to freedom and respect.

As ministers, canonists must be acutely conscious of the ideological slants and prejudices of the societies within which the churches live. They must struggle to promote authentic Christian values, whether the politicosocial conditions are congenial or inimical to those values. Genuine gospel teaching must be proclaimed in political contexts that are favorable as well as in those that are adverse. It is tempting and sometimes advantageous to curry favor with political leaders, but to do so a price must be paid, as civil officials frequently try to use the churches for their own purposes.

Canonists are responsible for the authentic function of ecclesial activities, even when the political ethos militates against it. The people's active participation in every phase of the life of their churches, including open communications and consultations, must be protected and encouraged even when governments attempt to repress it.

Economic Conditions

Economic systems and economic conditions also shape the culture and hence become vital factors for the churches. The economy, its structure and strength, qualifies nearly every aspect of human existence. Socialist economies with their planned, controlled, and supportive social systems offer sharp contrast to free market, laissez-faire capitalist economies. The presuppositions and mind-sets which these economic systems engender in people lead to quite different expectations of the government, in terms of taxation and assistance.

These attitudes and expectations regarding the economy "rub off" on church communities and affect their welfare just as the government's direct actions do. For example, some governments provide forms of financial assistance for churches or church-related institutions (e.g., Italy, Germany, Canada), while others do not. This in turn leads to very different expectations on the part of the churches regarding their support from lay contributions.

Economic conditions, both short- and long-term, cause even more dramatic results for peoples and their religious communities. Local Catholic churches live in starkly different conditions in wealthy, developed nations, like the United States, Germany, and

England, compared to those in woefully poor, undeveloped nations, like Belize, Bolivia, Burundi, and the Philippines. In the former, the upper socioeconomic group lives in affluence, with abundant goods and services, and conspicuous consumerism, alongside an underclass that subsists in relative poverty, malnourished, ill-housed, medically neglected, debt-ridden, and underemployed. In the underdeveloped nations conditions can be more uniformly wretched with bare subsistence, even starvation, rampant disease, high rates of illiteracy and infant mortality, and economies bereft of resources.

The churches, because they are communities of the people, share these starkly contrasting economic conditions. While all local Catholic churches maintain their identities as communities wherein the gospel is preached, sacramental worship is celebrated, and a communion of love and Christian witness is sustained, the conditions under which they do these things are radically diverse.

The churches' facilities, programs, ministers, and resources range from very primitive to the lavishly elaborate. Annual parish budgets vary from the equivalent of a few hundred dollars (often supplied from outside the community) to several million dollars (donated annually by the parishioners). Mass is regularly celebrated out of doors or in open sheds in some places, while in others it is held in large and ornate cathedrals.

All Catholic ministers are responsible for reminding their churches of the gospel's preferential option for the poor, especially in economic circumstances wherein "the rich are getting richer and the poor are getting poorer." The words of James' letter must be frequently repeated:

My brothers and sisters, show no partiality as you adhere to the faith in our glorious Lord Jesus Christ. For if one with gold rings on his fingers and in fine clothes comes into your assembly, and a poor person in shabby clothes also comes in, and you pay attention to the one with fine clothes and say, "Sit here, please," while you say to the poor one, "Stand there," or "Sit at my feet," have you not made distinctions among yourselves and becomes judges with evil designs? (2, 1–4)

The canonist has special obligations to see that "the perfect law of freedom"[1] is carried out in practice, because the canonist shares a particular responsibility for the structural relations within and among the local churches. Within each congregation provision must be made for the poor, and their needs met to the extent possible. This should be so not only in emergencies or when someone comes begging, but on a sustained basis and in a dignified manner. And among the churches, especially between wealthy and impoverished communities, within the same diocese or in different parts of the world, there must be similar, structured channels for steady supplies of assistance.

Paul's collection for the impoverished community in Jerusalem, although motivated by grace and love, was primarily a sign and function of Christian communion:

> Not that others should have relief while you are burdened, but that as a matter of equality your surplus at the present time should supply their needs, so that their surplus may also supply your needs, that there may be equality. As it is written (in the Book of Exodus about the manna gathered in the desert): "Whoever had much did not have more, and whoever had little did not have less."[2]

The event suggests a sense of mutuality and sharing which is ongoing, an interdependence within the communion of churches which cannot be shrugged off or forgotten.

Today this mutual assistance calls for structured expression and organized encouragement, and not only through the Holy See, but also by direct exchange between local churches. The canonist, aware of this aspect of ecclesial of communion, should facilitate such exchanges.

St. Mary's on Main Street, like most North American parishes, is well between the extremes of affluence and poverty, but its budget feels the pinch of its aging population with their declining incomes. Still the community cherishes its supportive ties to a needy parish in Guatemala.

Religious Context

The religious makeup of the larger society within which local Catholic churches exist is another factor of cultural influence. The religious convictions or attitudes of the people can reinforce and support the values and activities of church congregations, or they can impede and thwart them. The churches' own reactions and responses to their religious environments even affect their own identity and vitality.

Consider these four contrasting religious situations, as examples:

1) An overwhelmingly Catholic context wherein the vast majority of the population is at least nominally Catholic, as in Brazil, Ireland, Italy, Poland, or Spain. In such cultures not only can the churches live and operate freely, but many elements of the surrounding culture reflect and reinforce Catholic faith and practice.

2) A dominantly Christian milieu, but one in which Catholicism is one among many Christian churches and religious groups, as in the United States, Britain, Germany, or Australia. There are many opportunities for rivalry and conflict between religious forces as well as opportunities for agreement and cooperation. The culture may be less reinforcing, but it may actually promote clearer identities within churches.

3) Non-Christian contexts in which Christians are a tiny minority and may be barely tolerated by the religious majority, as for example in Muslim nations like Algeria, Syria, Pakistan, or Saudi Arabia. Public manifestations of Christian faith and any kind of evangelization are forbidden and social pressures militate against conversions, yet the church communities may be close-knit and strong because of the relative adversity of their situation.

4) Secular environments wherein all religions are viewed with suspicion or disfavor, either as "opiates of the people" or dangerously subversive, as in China, Turkey, or Albania. Here the local churches may be tolerated or even persecuted. They may survive, but they hardly thrive.

There are many more complex religious situations than these four examples. The point is that the religious environment within which the local churches live exerts pressures or brings benefits which pervasively affect the freedom, growth, and even the very self-concept of the communities of faith.

One would expect that an officially recognized established church, favored and supported by the state, would necessarily flourish, but such is not the case. On the other hand, one might expect minority congregations, barely tolerated and subject to discrimination, to wither and die out, but that too is not necessarily so.

Canonists must be aware of and well informed about the religious context of their churches. They can help interpret Catholic tradition and practices to the larger society around them. They must protect the legitimate rights of Catholic congregations, and weigh the impact of the surrounding religious culture on those communities.

Canonists must be ecumenists. They are to be leaders in fostering "the restoration of unity among all Christians which the Church is bound by the will of Christ to promote."[3] Likewise canonists must lead the churches in pursuing greater understanding and promoting positive relationships with non-Christians,[4] always upholding the principles of religious freedom.[5]

Geographic Location

Geography also subtly affects the culture within which churches exist. The physical context helps to define the people and, therefore, their faith communities. People think and act differently depending on where they live and work—in remote mountain valleys, in busy seaports, in arid deserts, in great river valleys, in forests and jungles, on vast fertile plains. All of these settings affect the outlook and prospects of the people as well as their view of life with God.

The location of congregations within major urban areas, in smaller cities and towns, in rural villages or crossroads, makes a big difference in their lives and activities. Even within huge urban complexes like New York, São Paulo, London, Mexico City, and Paris, the differences between life in the slums, ghettos, and favelas on the one hand and the affluent suburbs or exclusive neighborhoods on the other are drastic, often cruelly sharp. Even the location of a church on this side of town rather than the other, or in this neighborhood instead of another, makes a huge difference in its life and activities. These geographic settings impinge on the inner life of church communities, the members' ability to know one another, to interact with and assist one another. In other words, geography affects the very fabric of community life.

In some cultures the frequent movement of families from one location to another (migrant workers, military personnel, corporate executives) as well as the deterioration or restoration of whole neighborhoods also contributes greatly to the "life cycle" of local churches. In other places, the rootedness or "placedness" in a particular physical location and geographical setting is an integral part of the reality of the local congregation.

St. Mary's has been on Main Street for over one hundred years, but many of its newer members are recent Vietnamese immigrants from rural villages. The community has welcomed them, but they are not yet fully at home in this new environment.

History

History is at the heart of culture. The movements and struggles, triumphs and sufferings, over the whole course of a people's history is what makes them a distinct people. Mexicans, Germans, Irish, Slovaks, Hutus, and Tutsis—all are defined by their corporate histories. However, in addition to the sweep of the common history of a people, the story of each *local* community also distinguishes and identifies it.

Each congregation has a history of its own. The story of this particular Catholic parish needs to be learned and relearned. How long have they been here? When did they migrate, from where? What farm crop or coal mine or manufacturing industry drew them? What war or famine or persecution caused their flight? How were they received in their new home? Did they have to provide their own presbyter, their own house of worship and programs of formation? How did their earlier history differ from the present?

Each local church, especially each parish community, has its own history. Each must remember its own story, and strive to make it a part of its present life and future plans. Patterns of growth and decline, of building and rebuilding, of mergers and compromises, of achievements and failures, all need to be recorded and recounted. Only by recalling and retelling this narrative can the community take justifiable pride in what it is and what it has accomplished.

The community's history is ongoing, it extends into the future. Families grow up and move away. New people come into the neighborhood, and become part of the community, sometimes with ease, sometimes with resistance. A new majority emerges with new leadership and new challenges arise and new projects are launched. In a hundred years, a parish may have transformed itself several times, yet the community continues.

Maintaining an accurate history of local churches should be a canonical requirement, just as the careful preservation of their sacramental records is.[6] The events of the community's life deserve the same careful recording as those of the individuals. Oral histories and narratives reverence the lives of the faithful people as do the written records of the milestones: special celebrations, anniversaries, changes in leadership, minutes of meetings. The canonist cannot be the archivist, much less the chronicler, of every local congregation, but she or he can take care that their histories are not lost.

Education

Educational level is another key component of culture. Vibrant Catholic communities exist in which most of the members are completely illiterate, and equally vital churches have members whose average educational level is graduate school. Their depth of faith, the quality of their Christian lives, and even their fundamental wisdom and prudence may not be distinguishable, but the preaching, catechesis, formation, and decision-making processes within them are probably quite different.

Congregations in which there is a great diversity of educational backgrounds have their own problems with communications. Some segments of the parish mix are "turned off" when announcements are aimed "over their heads."

The level of academic achievement, which often goes hand in hand with socioeconomic status, is not an indicator of Christian love or witness, but it is an important human factor which must be taken into consideration by the ministers and other members of the local church.

Sometimes both ministers and their parishioners experience difficulty and frustration in trying to understand one another. Differences in educational background, like differences in language and ethnic origins, can complicate life, conversation, and ministry within local churches.

The canonist must keep in mind the levels of education of the communities served and the ministers assigned or chosen to serve them. And the canonist must make the necessary adjustments, in applying and explaining the church's rules, for those who are simple and unlettered as well as for those who are highly educated and cosmopolitan.

Employment

Employment, the means by which people make their living, is another distinguishing feature of local communities of the faithful. "White collar" or "blue collar" are broad categories often used to describe parishes. But there are many more specific categories of employment (or unemployment) which indicate what kind of community it is and what kind of lives the people lead. Farmers, government workers (from trash collectors to executives), laborers in the building trades, service workers, professionals (doctors, lawyers, nurses, managers) are among the many categories of employment.

Some local churches consist mainly of retired persons. Others are located where large numbers of people take their holiday vacations or there is a seasonal influx of migrant workers. When one of these employment categories predominates in a local church, as sometimes happens when nearly all the breadwinners work in one factory or mine or industry, it makes a great difference in the congregation. It colors the attitudes and expectations which the people have toward the congregation and its leadership. It influences the time and talents which the people can contribute to the parish.

For example, in some churches most adults could serve effectively on the finance council, while in others few could offer much help in financial or administrative matters. Conversely, some communities have many skilled workers (carpenters, painters, technicians), and others have almost none. There may be scores of good teachers in some congregations, and very few in others. Such occurrences as strikes, lockouts, layoffs, and plant closings can devastate the morale as well as the finances of a congregation.

In Conclusion

The foregoing factors both constitute and identify the human situation of local churches. They also differentiate them and point up their diversity. These human features distinctively shape each parish and make it unique within the larger communion.

Local congregations are plants that combine to make a garden. Each has its own culture and beauty, its own weaknesses and strengths. No one is precisely the same as another, and their very diversity and interplay creates the glory of God's garden.

The canonist, who strives to preserve Christian freedom and maintain good order, must always be acutely aware of the "situation," the cultural context of each church. Congregations cannot all be treated just the same because they are not all just the same. The unique character of each parish compels the canonist to listen, attend, and minister to each one with understanding, fairness, and love.

PARTICULARITIES OF PLACE: PRINCIPLES

In addition to the cultural factors which help to define local churches, there are two social principles which contribute to their identities. These operative principles are drawn from Catholic social teaching, and they represent two very real influences on the lives of local communities. They are:1) the principle of subsidiary function, and 2) the principle of solidarity.

Subsidiarity

Subsidiarity implies an appropriate autonomy and self-direction for the local church. The local congregation is always committed to the communion of churches, those nearby, others in the diocese, and all those within the communion of the universal church. But, at the same time, the local congregation possesses its own identity, its proper responsibilities, and its legitimate freedom of action.

Pope Pius XI articulated the principle of subsidiarity in his landmark encyclical on the reconstruction of the social order.[7] He described it as "that most weighty principle, which cannot be set aside or changed, [and which] remains fixed and unshaken in social philosophy":

> Just as it is gravely wrong to take from individuals what they can accomplish by their own initiative and industry and give it to the community, so also it is an injustice and at the same time a grave evil and disturbance of right order to assign to a greater and higher association what lesser and subordinate organizations can do. For every social activity ought of its very nature to furnish help to the members of the body social, and never destroy and absorb them. (*QA* 79)

Pope John XXIII repeated the definition in *Mater et magistra*[8] and called it the "guiding principle of subsidiary function" (*MM* 53). Pope John Paul II restated the principle again in 1991:[9]

Here again the principle of subsidiarity must be respected. A community of a higher order should not interfere in the internal life of a community of a lower order, depriving the latter of its functions, but rather should support it in case of need and help to coordinate its activity with the activities of the rest of society, always with a view to the common good. (*CA* 48)

The application of this principle *within the church,* as well as within the larger society, has been repeatedly affirmed by the church's own authorities.[10] In 1967 the principle of subsidiarity was formally adopted by the Synod of Bishops as one of the principles to guide the revision of the Code of Canon Law: "Careful attention is to be given to the greater application of the principle of subsidiarity within the Church."[11]

What does the principle of subsidiarity mean for the local church? It strongly accentuates the legitimate autonomy of the local community of the faithful in relationship to the diocese and other wider communities. It means that the parish has a right to continue in existence with a maximum of self-direction and appropriate initiatives and activities. Canonically this truth is reaffirmed by the fact that each parish is a juridic person, perpetual by nature, from the time of its establishment.

Subsidiarity does not imply a complete autonomy or independence from the diocesan bishop. Local churches must always remain in communion with the bishop and with the other churches which make up the diocesan church. The diocese, however, should support, assist, and coordinate the activities of parishes and other local communities. It is not for the diocese to dominate them, micro-manage them, or subsume their activities.

Solidarity

Solidarity signals the connectedness within the community, the sense of interdependence which links its members together. It is a measure of the people's commitment to participate in the life of the community and to promote its common good.

While solidarity has long been an implicit principle in Catholic social teaching, it was Pope John Paul II who explicitly articulated the notion of solidarity in an encyclical in 1987:[12]

> It is above all a question of interdependence, sensed as a system determining relationships in the contemporary world, in its economic, cultural, political and religious elements, and accepted as a moral category. When interdependence becomes recognized in this way, the correlative response as a moral and social attitude, as a "virtue," is solidarity. This is not a feeling of vague compassion or shallow distress at the misfortunes of people....On the contrary, it is a firm and persevering determination to commit oneself to the common good; that is to say, to the good of all and of each individual because we are all really responsible for all. (*SRS* 38.4)

Solidarity is a sense of mutual responsibility and care, based on a recognition of human interdependence. It has application locally, within the community of believers, as well as globally, within the community of nations.

> The exercise of solidarity within each society is valid when its members recognize each other as persons. (*SRS* 39)

> Solidarity helps us to see the "other"...not just as some kind of instrument...but as our "neighbor," as our "helper" (cf. Gen 2, 18–20), to be made a sharer on a par with ourselves in the banquet of life to which all are equally invited by God. (*SRS* 39.4)

Solidarity is the fiber that holds congregations together. It is part of their very texture. It helps to define local churches as communities wherein people's lives are intertwined and mutually dependent.

Solidarity especially obliges attention to the needs of the weak and disadvantaged within the community as well as of those farther away. However, solidarity means much more than "chicken soup neighborliness." It goes beyond simple charity to a recognition of the *right* of the other to be at the table, to be a full participant in every facet of community life.

In Conclusion

Situational factors, which are the elements of human culture, are more than descriptors. They are more than labels that tell how one local church differs from another. These factors constitute the reality of the human community, which is also a graced community of faith, hope, and love. As such, they are part of the very nature of local church.

At St. Mary's on Main Street, when the ministers and members of the parish want to understand and interpret their own community, they begin by recalling these elements of place and roots, of situation and history. Then they remind themselves of the social principles of subsidiarity and solidarity which undergird their rightful dignity as a parish.

Canonists are guided in their ministry by canonical rules. They are obliged to interpret and apply the church's canons, as well as to search for better ones. But at another level canonists are guided by the theology that tells them what the church is and what it is for, and by the specific situation of each one of its local communities. These are the two essential contexts for canonical ministry: a theological vision and the local situation.

CHAPTER 5

FREEDOM IN THE CHURCH:
FIRST FOCUS OF THE MINISTRY
OF THE CANONIST

FREEDOM IS A POLESTAR FOR THE CHURCH, and canonists must always keep it in view. The canonist strives for many values: unity, reconciliation, justice, integrity of word and sacrament, the breath of the Spirit. But it is Christian freedom that is salient and overarching.

This thesis about freedom in the church has nothing to do with liberalism as over against conservatism or fundamentalism. It has nothing to do with the "free church tradition," that is, the heritage of nonestablished churches like Congregationalists, Quakers, Methodists, or Baptists. And it certainly has nothing to do with left-leaning policies or lax observance. It is not even about liberation theology. Freedom here has everything to do with the radical basis of the Christian calling, and the nature and purpose of the church.

The ministry of the canonist, besides enabling good order and the exercise of authority as service, is to safeguard freedom in the church. The canonist is to keep watch over the churches to see that freedom is secure in them, just as the gardener carefully scrutinizes flower beds for weeds or blights or pests which might harm or hinder the growth of the plants. The canonist is to be on the lookout for incursions of unfreedom: domination, despotism, coercion, intimidation, and control that stifles the Spirit. The canonist is to assure that the church is "a protected zone of freedom."

For the purpose of this ministry, it is essential to know the parameters of Christian freedom. What follows is a brief exploration of those parameters: 1) freedom in Christ, 2) religious freedom, 3) primacy of conscience, 4) power of discretion, 5) discernment of the Spirit, 6) rights of persons and communities in the church, 7) inculturation, 8) churches as voluntary associations.

FREEDOM IN CHRIST

The New Testament teaching on "the glorious freedom of the children of God" (Rom 8, 21) is loud and clear. This shining facet of Christ's redeeming message has been partially obscured in recent centuries. The Catholic Church's reactions to the Protestant Reformation and to modern political liberalism (after the French Revolution) caused Catholic theology to downplay the pristine teaching on Christian freedom. A robust theology of the *libertas christiana* was replaced by a narrow focus on the interaction of grace and free will. The theological revival, epitomized by the Second Vatican Council, has raised up the original splendor of this truth.

The Gospel of John records Jesus' teaching in the context of a polemical discourse:

> "If you remain in my word, you will truly be my disciples, and you will know the truth, and the truth will make you free." They (the Jews to whom Jesus was speaking) answered him, "We are descendants of Abraham and have never been enslaved to anyone. How can you say, 'You will become free'?" Jesus answered them, "Amen, amen, I say to you, everyone who commits sin is a slave of sin....If the son frees you, you will truly be free." (Jn 8, 31–36)

The "word" of which Jesus spoke is the revelation that the Son of God has brought, which is the "truth," the reliable rule of life. It sets free those who accept it, believe in it, and live by it. It sets them free from their slavery or attachment to sin. When

Jesus described the freedom of the children of God he contrasted the freedom proper to the child of the family to the bondage of the slave.

For Paul, freedom is one way of characterizing the saving action of Christ. He had in mind both the free status of a child born of a free woman as over against the subjugated condition of one born of a slave,[1] and the status of a fully empowered citizen of a Greek city-state or of a Roman citizen (which, of course, Paul himself was; Acts 22). The difference between a free person and a slave in both contexts was real, dramatic, and stark, just as it was in the cruel history of Africa and the Americas. Deliverance from the enslaved condition was well recognized and held life-changing implications. For Paul and his hearers "slavery and freedom" was not a literary metaphor, it was a vivid part of real life.

"For freedom Christ has set us free; so stand firm and do not again submit to the yoke of slavery" (Gal 5, 1). Paul referred to freedom from the Mosaic law, from sin, and from death. "The law of the spirit of life in Christ Jesus has freed you from the law of sin and death" (Rom 8, 2). The presence of the Holy Spirit guarantees Christian freedom. "Where the Spirit of the Lord is, there is freedom" (2 Cor 3, 17).

This freedom achieved for us by Christ has a future dimension as well as an ongoing challenge. All of the created universe will one day share in an eschatological liberation. "For creation awaits with eager expectation the revelation of the children of God...in hope that creation itself would be set free from slavery to corruption and share in the glorious freedom of the children of God" (Rom 8, 19–21). The present task for Christians is to live up to this freed status and not to betray or forsake it:

> For you were called for freedom, sisters and brothers. But do not use this freedom as an opportunity for the flesh; rather serve one another through love. For the whole law is fulfilled in one statement, namely, "You shall love your neighbor as yourself." (Gal 5, 13–14)

For Paul, then, the Christian vocation is a call to liberty. It means being led by the Spirit in life and action, freed from the constant constraint of extrinsic forces or norms. Some members of the earliest Pauline and Johannine communities were tempted to revert to some of the external observances of the Mosaic law. But for later generations of Christians the temptation has often been to substitute conformity to church regulations for obedience to the law of the Spirit.

The law of the Spirit is the "new law," the law of grace, and is identified with the presence and activity of the Spirit within us. That is, the law of the Spirit is not a new set of norms outside us, but a new source of energy, a dynamism within us. This is the "law" that is life-giving, the "observance" which leads to salvation.

The Epistle of James refers to this saving word of Christ as "the perfect law of liberty" (Jas 1, 25). It should make Christians "doers of the word" and not self-deluded hearers only. Peering into this "law of liberty" should lead to action. Reflecting on it should free true disciples to carry out the law in practice, to care for orphans and widows, to show mercy, and in doing so to obtain God's blessing.

Jesus railed against those who idolized external observances, especially the fine points of the law, and urged religious burdens on others.

> Oh you Pharisees! Although you cleanse the outside of the cup and the dish, inside you are plunder and evil....You pay tithes of mint and of rue and of every garden herb, but you pay no attention to judgment and to love for God....Woe to you scholars of the law! You impose on people burdens hard to carry, but you yourselves do not lift one finger to touch them. (Lk 11, 39–46)

The earliest churches seem to have tried to minimize external religious obligations, mindful of the Lord's admonitions and harkening to the Spirit's bidding. An instance occurred at the resolution of the major conflict over the need for the followers of Christ to observe the law of circumcision as necessary for salvation. A gathering of the apostles and presbyters "in agreement with the whole church" sent a message to the church at Antioch. According to Luke, this "Council of Jerusalem" declared, "It is the decision of the Holy Spirit and of us not to place on you any burden beyond that which is strictly necessary" (Acts 15, 28). Having made a negative judgment about the need for circumcision, they then included, in summary form, three provisions of Mosaic law[2] minimally necessary for common life in the mixed Jewish-Gentile Christian community in Antioch. The community there received the message with delight (15, 31).

This freedom in Christ is integral to the Christian vocation and striving. It does not pretend that Christ's followers are not capable of sin, nor that they do not need rules. Freedom does not permit Christians to disregard possible scandal given to others. Paul carefully explained about eating meat which had been offered to idols: "All things are lawful...does not mean that everything is constructive" (1 Cor 10, 23–33).

Freedom is central to the new law, the law of grace. It is not only freedom *from* an old law which provoked transgressions, it is a freedom *for* service and love. Christians have been set free to love one another in Christ, to "love one another as I have loved you" (Jn 15, 12). The church itself must always harken to the declaration that, "where the Spirit of the Lord is, there is freedom" (2 Cor 3, 17).

This Christian liberty is corporate, communal, as well as individual and personal. Communities of believers, both local and particular churches, are to witness to Christ's love and redemptive message to the world around them. The life of the community is visible. So at St. Mary's on Main Street the congregation's conduct and actions should prompt the observation, "See how they really live *with* one another in *freedom* and with as few constraints as possible."[3]

RELIGIOUS FREEDOM

The Roman Catholic Church embraced the principle of religious liberty at the Second Vatican Council. This dramatic action was a major milestone in the history of the church. The *Declaration on Religious Freedom* was a turnabout, a volte-face so notable as to constitute a classic example of the development of doctrine.

The church, after spending its youth as a minority religion in uneasy relationship with the Roman Empire, grew up and came of age as an established church, on comfortable terms with governmental authority. The church not only had "friends in high places," like emperors, kings, and princes, but it often occupied the privileged position of "the religion of the state." While the church had argued passionately for its own freedom to exist in Roman times, for about twelve hundred years, from the Peace of Constantine to the Protestant Reformation, it enjoyed a virtual religious monopoly, at least in most of Europe. In this long period of official favor, it developed an attitude which barely tolerated other religions, and was outright hostile to both "heretics" and nonbelievers.

The change in official public policy at the Council was preceded by many decades of reflection on human rights, on the dignity of the human person, and on the successful life and growth of the church under conditions of religious freedom. In other words, the church's experiences, both negative and positive, of religious liberty since the Enlightenment finally came to reflective maturity, and caused a basic alteration in teaching.

The church's conviction about religious freedom is based squarely on the nature of the human person and on the nature of religion. That is what makes the teaching so significant for the internal life of the church. It is not a mere expedient, a better strategy for dealing with contemporary secular authorities. Rather it derives from the very conditions of human existence and of Christian belief, as seen in the light of reason and of divine revelation. The texts of the *Declaration* should be examined:

> This Vatican synod declares that the human person has a right to religious freedom. Such freedom consists in this, that all should have such immunity from coercion by individuals, or by groups, or by any human power, that no one should be forced to act against his (or her) conscience in religious matters, nor prevented from acting according to conscience,

whether in private or in public, whether alone or in association with others, within due limits. The synod further declares that the right to religious freedom is firmly based on the dignity of the human person as this is known from the revealed word of God and from reason itself. (*DH* 2)

In accordance with their dignity as persons, equipped with reason and free will and endowed with personal responsibility, all are impelled by their own nature and are bound by a moral obligation to seek truth, above all religious truth....But people are only able to meet this obligation in ways that accord with their own nature, if they enjoy both psychological freedom and freedom from external coercion. This right to religious freedom is based on human nature itself, and not on any merely personal attitude of mind. (*DH* 2)

The practice of religion of its very nature consists principally in internal acts which are voluntary and free, in which one relates oneself to God directly; and these can neither be commanded nor prevented by any merely human power. The social nature of human beings, however, requires that they should express these interior religious acts externally, share their religion with others, and witness to it communally. (*DH* 3)

The liberty or freedom from coercion in religion which is proper to all persons must also be allowed them when they act together (*in communi agentibus*). (*DH* 4)

The *Declaration* goes on to show that the firm bases for religious freedom, both personal and communal, are found in revelation as well as in human reason. The radical freedom of the act of faith is a central Christian tenet. That is, the response of human persons to God's self-revelation and invitation to become God's adoptive children through Jesus Christ must be both reasonable and free (*DH* 10). God calls humankind to serve him in spirit and in truth, by personal choice, and not as a result of any sort of external coercion. This is how Christ acted with his own disciples, and how he instructed them to proclaim the gospel to the world. The apostles followed the same course of action in their efforts to convert men and women to Christ, not by any kind of force, but solely by the power of God's message (*DH* 11).

> Hence the church is being faithful to the truth of the gospel and is following the way of Christ and the apostles, when it sees the principle of religious freedom as in accord with human dignity and the revelation of God, and when it promotes it. (*DH* 12)

The Council's *Declaration on Religious Freedom* was directed primarily to civil authorities; it was a statement of the church's own freedom within society as well as the liberty owed to all other religious bodies. However, the teaching has unmistakable implications for the church's own inner life and operations. The same respect, forbearance, and freedom to search for truth that the church demands from civil governments must be shown within the church itself.

> Hence this Vatican synod exhorts all, and particularly those who have the charge of educating others, to apply themselves to bringing up people who will respect the moral law, obey legitimate authority and have a love for genuine freedom; that is, people who will use their own judgment to make decisions in the light of truth, plan their activities with a sense of responsibility, and freely combine their efforts with others to achieve all that is just and true. (*DH* 8)

Local churches, including parishes and other Catholic congregations, and dioceses, should be characterized by this same authentic spirit of freedom in religious matters.

PRIMACY OF CONSCIENCE

Personal conscience is another "zone of freedom" which the churches are obliged to protect. The Second Vatican Council forcefully restated the crucial role of conscience in Christian moral decision-making. The Council's teaching affirmed the Catholic tradition on conscience, more than it developed it. The position might better be described as the "ultimacy" of personal conscience, rather than its "primacy."

> Deep within their conscience individuals discover a law which they do not make for themselves but which they are bound to obey, whose voice, ever summoning them to love and do what is good and to avoid what is evil, rings in their hearts when necessary with the command: Do this, keep away from that. For inscribed in their hearts by God, human beings have a law whose observance is their dignity and in accordance with which they are to be judged. Conscience is the most intimate center and sanctuary of a person, in which he or she is alone with God whose voice echoes within them. (*GS* 16)

> People grasp and acknowledge the precepts of the divine law by means of their own consciences, which they are bound to follow faithfully in all their activity so as to come to God, their end. (*DH* 3)

Here the Council sounded the teaching of the Apostle Paul on the interior law. He said that the Gentiles, who observed the prescriptions of the Mosaic law which was not given to them, "show that the demands of the law are written in their hearts." Thus their consciences will bear witness for them when God judges their hidden works through Christ Jesus (Rom 2, 14–16).

For consciences to be true guides, whose works are worthy of praise or blame, they must perforce be free.

> It is only in freedom, however, that human beings can turn to what is good....Genuine freedom is an outstanding manifestation of the divine image in humans. For God willed to leave them in the hands of their own counsel, so that they would seek their creator of their own accord and would freely arrive at full and blessed perfection by cleaving to God. Their human dignity therefore requires them to act through conscious and free choice, as motivated and prompted personally from within, and not through blind internal impulse or merely external pressure. (*GS* 17)

They must therefore not be forced to act against their conscience. Nor must they be prevented from acting according
to it, especially in religious matters. (*DH* 3)[4]

Conscience is not so much an isolated "faculty" or "power"
within the human person, as it is the person herself or himself, as
morally conscious and morally responsible. It is the person striving to respond to multiple relationships, with others and with
God. Conscience describes the human subject as moral agent,
searching and reaching toward values, toward authenticity and
self-transcendence in the context of these relationships.

In this vision of conscience and its operation, or even in a
more traditional, facultative scheme,[5] conscience is always the
ultimate norm of moral action, and, as such: a) it must be
formed, b) it must be followed, and c) it must be free.

a) Each person has the obligation continually and properly
to form her or his conscience, by training, reflection, dialogue,
and prayer. Formation of conscience is part of the ongoing task
of Christian conversion. It takes place within the individual communities which comprise the church. Personal limitations and
sinful inclinations are more readily overcome in the context of a
community.

b) Likewise, one must decide and act in accord with one's
own conscience. In this sense conscience is the final norm of
morality. One must be true to oneself in order to be authentically Christian. Each person, as an acting subject, must accept
the freedom and responsibility which God has given her or him.

c) Constrained conscience cannot command truly moral
activity. If there is no choice to be made, no range of human freedom, then there is no conscientious action, no opportunity for
virtue or vice. A coerced compliance or an externally compelled
conscience is no conscience at all.

The communities within the church, at every level, must strive
to provide freedom to their members in their moral formation and
decision-making, otherwise there is no real following of Christ. The
church communities should be healthy contexts in which mature
Christian consciences are supported and can function freely.

In addition, decisions of local churches must emerge from a collective or "community conscience." Communities, like individuals, are obliged to act conscientiously. They possess a shared moral sense, an estimation of moral values in the context of the pragmatic decision at hand. It is not the same as personal conscience, but it is analogous. And the "conscience of the community" has the same need to be carefully formed and exercised in freedom.

At St. Mary's on Main Street decisions are not made hastily, but they are made conscientiously. The community and its councils allow opportunity for discernment before decisions are made. They encourage the expression of differing views and weigh the values within their options. They take their time, pray, discuss, and decide, and, in doing so, they try to follow the conscience of the community.

POWER OF DISCRETION

One of the elements of freedom is the ability to make choices. Where there are no options, no alternatives from which to choose, there is not much room for freedom. When the process for the revision of the *Code* began after the Second Vatican Council, a set of "principles to direct the revision process" was drawn up by the Commission for Revision and given formal approval at the 1967 Synod of Bishops.[6] One of the principles was to leave to bishops and others charged with the care of souls "a suitable discretionary authority" *(congrua potestas discretionis)* in determining the duties of the faithful and evaluating individual situations, as was done in the Apostolic Constitution on Fast and Abstinence.[7]

The power of discretion means the ability or freedom to decide and act according to one's own judgment, to discern a course of action, at least within a range of options. The power was recommended as an exercise of subsidiary function, of flexibility, and of adaptation.

At the time the work of revision was nearing its conclusion, Pope Paul VI reiterated this principle and extended it to the faithful in these words:

The purpose of the entire array of laws is to help the faithful in their spiritual life, which must be inspired by personal conscience and a sense of responsibility rather than by precepts.

Therefore, the canonical norms are not to impose obligations whenever it is clear that instruction, exhortation, persuasion and other methods of fostering the communion of the faithful are adequate to achieve the church's purpose....

The same principles (which guided the revision, especially that of pastoral care) seem to require that a suitable discretionary authority *(congrua potestas discretionalis)* be left to pastors and faithful.[8]

Pope Paul reminded the canonical drafters that the end or purpose of the new *Code* was to assist the faithful to lead Christian lives. People would succeed in doing that, not by obedience to external laws, but by following their own consciences, by taking responsibility for their own lives. So, in offering guidance to them, the canons should respect their power of discretion, their need to make their own discernment of what is best for their following of Christ.

The example which the pope held out to the canonists was the Constitution on Penance, which he had issued shortly after the close of the Second Vatican Council.[9] The document completely revised the Catholic discipline of fasting and abstinence. It is a model for rule-making within the church. The heart of the Constitution explained the scriptural basis for penance, the example of Christ himself, and the tradition of the church. It spoke of the preeminence of interior and religious penance, the need for some external expression of the virtue, and cautioned of the dangers of formalism and phariseeism.

Then, in a brief dispositive section, the Constitution invited the faithful "to accompany the inner conversion of the spirit with the voluntary exercise of external acts of penance," in keeping with their circumstances and condition of life. It left further specification to episcopal conferences "in their pastoral solicitude and prudence, and with the direct knowledge they have of local conditions." In keeping with the principle of subsidiarity, the document showed ample regard for the appropriate power of discretion of both pastors and people.

This "appropriate power of discretion" is a key part of the freedom which must characterize life within the church. At St. Mary's on Main Street, when action is to be taken on policies or programs, the community tries to explore the full range of its options so as to exercise its own proper power of discretion.

DISCERNMENT OF THE SPIRIT

The followers of Christ, individually and in their communities, are to be guided by the Holy Spirit. "Those who are led by the Spirit of God are the children of God" (Rom 8, 14). "I say, then: live by the Spirit...if you are guided by the Spirit" (Gal 5, 16 and 18). "Whoever has ears ought to hear what the Spirit says to the churches" (Rev 2, 7). "Do not quench the Spirit" (1 Thes 5, 19). To seek and search out the guidance of the Holy Spirit is a fundamental freedom and duty of all Christians.

The Spirit's guidance does not come in the form of written messages, direct address, or personal revelation. Sometimes it occurs in the context of intense religious experience, which raises the dangers of subjectivity, self-deception, or overexcited enthusiasm. Because of these dangers and the inherent ambiguity of religious experiences, from the very beginning Christians have seen the need of discernment. "Test everything; retain what is good. Refrain from every kind of evil" (1 Thes 5 21–22). "Beloved, do not trust every spirit but test the spirits to see whether they belong to God, because many false prophets have gone out into the world" (1 Jn 4, 1). It is for this "testing of spirits" that churches are given the spiritual gift which Paul named "the discernment of spirits" (1 Cor 12, 10).

Discernment, then, can refer to the charismatic gift, or to a connatural sensitivity, or to a learned ability, or to all three. It makes little difference whether, in discerning the value of religious impulses, one searches for the source of the inspiration, that is, whether it comes from good or evil spirits, or whether one looks for the traces of the Holy Spirit, the "finger of God," on it.[10]

The early Christian communities worked out criteria by which to make these discernments. First, there was a threshold indicator, the faith in Christ that the bearer of the message professes: "I tell you that nobody speaking by the spirit of God says, 'Jesus be accursed.' And no one can say 'Jesus is Lord,' except by the Holy Spirit." [11] Their expressed conviction about Jesus Christ was the first test.

Then, in Matthew's church there was the clear "rule of results":

> Beware of false prophets, who come to you in sheep's clothing, but underneath are ravenous wolves. By their fruits you will know them. Do people pick grapes from thornbushes, or figs from thistles? Just so, every good tree bears good fruit, and a rotten tree bears bad fruit....So by their fruits you will know them. (Mt 7, 15-20)[12]

Paul's writings reveal a more detailed set of criteria for telling the "works of the flesh" from the "fruit of the Spirit":

> Now the works of the flesh are obvious: immorality, impurity, licentiousness, idolatry, sorcery, hatreds, rivalry, jealousy, outbursts of fury, acts of selfishness, dissensions, factions, occasions of envy, drinking bouts, orgies and the like.
>
> In contrast, the fruit of the Spirit is love, joy, peace, patience, kindness, generosity, faithfulness, gentleness, self-control. (Gal 5, 19-23)

The attitudes and actions of the persons or communities disclosed their orientation, whether or not they proceeded from the Spirit of God. Their behavior and moral stance was the sure measure of their authenticity.

Finally, there was the pattern of lives actually being directed by the Spirit. For example, the Acts of the Apostles detailed how Paul was set apart and sent forth (13, 4), compelled to travel (20, 22), and prevented from preaching (16, 6) "by the Holy Spirit." And the Spirit was seen to be acting in the church: making decisions (15, 28), consoling and giving growth (9, 31), and appointing overseers (20, 28). In specific choices and actions both individuals and local churches followed Paul's admonition, "If we live in the Spirit, let us also follow the Spirit" (Gal 5, 25).

In these New Testament contexts "discernment of spirits" was clearly both communal and personal, but the subsequent monastic tradition developed it in an individual direction. It tended to focus on a person's thoughts, choices, temptations, interior feelings, insights, and inclinations, and much less on ecclesial decisions, priorities, or policies. This use of discernment as a tool in the individual's spiritual life is clearly evident in the classic works of Origen, John Cassian, John Climacus, and Ignatius of Loyola.

The gift or skill of discernment needs to be returned to its communitarian function. It should be consciously brought to bear in answering questions like "How is the Spirit guiding our local church at this juncture?" It is a necessary part of the community's freedom and self-direction. Discernment is part of the decision-making process at St. Mary's on Main Street. It takes patience and sensitivity, testing and prayerful listening, but it gives the whole parish the assurance of trying to be in touch with the Spirit.

The Second Vatican Council moved discernment in this ecclesial direction by insisting on a Spirit-guided "discerning of the signs of the times." This formulation stems from the statement of Jesus that his hearers were quite able to read the signs of the next day's weather, but unable to see the signs of God's future for their world: "You know how to judge the appearance of the sky, but you cannot judge the signs of the times."[13] The *Pastoral Constitution on the Church in the Modern World* spoke this way of the church's need to discern:

> The church...has in mind...with the guidance of the Paraclete, to continue the work of Christ who came into the world to give witness to the truth, to save and not to judge, to serve and not to be served.

To discharge this function, the church has the duty in every age of examining the signs of the times and interpreting them in the light of the gospel. (*GS* 3 and 4)

Impelled by its belief that it is being led by the Spirit of the Lord who fills the whole earth, God's people works to discern the true signs of God's presence and purpose in the events, needs and desires which it shares with the rest of modern humanity. (*GS* 11).[14]

It is for God's people as a whole, with the help of the Holy Spirit, and especially for pastors and theologians, to listen to the various voices of our day, discerning them and interpreting them, and to evaluate them in the light of the divine word, so that the revealed truth can be increasingly appropriated, better understood and more suitably expressed. (*GS* 44)

The *Decree on the Ministry and Life of Priests* added:

[Priests] should readily listen to lay people,...recognizing their experience and competence in various fields of human activity, so as to join with them in reading the signs of the times *(ut simul cum ipsis signa temporum recognoscere queant).* They are to test the spirits to see whether they are of God, discern with a sense of faith the manifold gifts, both exalted and ordinary, that the laity have, acknowledge them gladly and foster them with care. (*PO* 9)

Pope Paul VI, writing on the occasion of the eightieth anniversary of the first modern social encyclical, applied this same teaching to the search for appropriate policies and actions in the area of social justice:

It is up to the Christian communities to analyze with objectivity the situation which is proper to their own country, to shed on it the light of the gospel's unalterable words, and to draw principles of reflection, norms of judgment and directives for action from the social teaching of the church....It is up to these Christian communities, with the help of the Holy Spirit, in communion with the bishops who hold responsibility and in dialogue with other Christians and all

persons of good will, to discern the options and commit-
ments which are called for in order to bring about the social,
political and economic changes seen in many cases to be
urgently needed.[15]

The 1974 Synod of Bishops, in its declaration on the evangelization of the modern world, returned to the theme of the
church's discernment of the signs of the times:

> We are profoundly convinced that without the grace of God,
> which is spread by the Father in our hearts through the Holy
> Spirit, we would be completely incapable of carrying out this
> mission as it should be done (cf. Rom 5, 5)....We will acquire
> the ability to discover and discern the signs of the times and
> to recognize and respect the action of the Spirit of Christ
> who is always at work in the life of the church itself and in all
> human history so that everyone may have the fullness of a
> better life.[16]

Discernment, in its biblical and modern senses, is clearly a
deliberate and vital ecclesial task, guided by the Holy Spirit, in
which all of the baptized participate in determining practical
courses of action. It is an integral component of freedom within
the church, for individuals and communities.

The process of discernment should always include protracted prayer, discretion, prudence (the virtue which enables
one to select and put into operation the most suitable means to
an end), critical reflection, group deliberation, appropriate consultation, and constant attention to divine revelation and the
Christian tradition.

RIGHTS OF PERSONS AND COMMUNITIES

The most obvious *canonical* sources for the parameters of
freedom within the Catholic communion are the contemporary
codes: the 1983 *Code of Canon Law* for the Latin Church, and the
1990 *Code of Canons for the Eastern Churches.* Both of these modern
codes contain a prominent section on the rights and obligations

of the Christian faithful.[17] The provisions of the two codes, which are nearly identical, are derived largely from the documents of the Second Vatican Council.

Individual Catholics, that is, those baptized Christians who are in full communion with the Catholic Church, enjoy a set of rights *(iura)* according to the canonical codes. These formulations of rights are another way of describing the freedoms of church members:

a) All of the Christian faithful are truly equal in their dignity and activity whereby all cooperate to build up the body of Christ.

b) All have the right to work to make the divine message of salvation reach all peoples.

c) The Christian faithful have the right to make their needs and desires known to the pastors of the church.

d) All have the right to make their opinions regarding the good of the church known to the pastors of the church and to the other Christian faithful.

e) All have the right to receive assistance from the pastors of the church, especially the word of God and the sacraments.

f) The Christian faithful have the right to worship God in their own rite and to follow their own form of spiritual life.

g) All have the right to found and direct associations for charitable or religious purposes or to promote the Christian vocation in the world, and the right to hold meetings for such purposes.

h) All have the right to initiate, promote, and sustain apostolic activities.

i) All of the Christian faithful have a right to Christian education, in order to develop human maturity and to know and live the mystery of salvation.

j) Those engaged in the theological disciplines enjoy freedom of inquiry and of expression of their opinions.

k) All have the right to be free from any kind of coercion in choosing their state of life.
l) No one is permitted to damage the good reputation of another nor to violate the right of others to protect their own privacy.
m) The Christian faithful have the right to vindicate and defend their rights before an ecclesiastical court.
n) If summoned to judgment by church authority, all have the right to be judged in accord with Canon Law applied with equity.
o) All have the right not to be canonically punished except in accordance with the law.

In the exercise of these rights the faithful are to take account of the common good of the church, of the rights of others, and of their own duties toward others. Church authorities, too, may regulate the exercise of these rights in the interest of the common good.

The right to exercise one's own gifts from the Holy Spirit, although curiously omitted from the canonical lists,[18] was a clear teaching of the Council:

> From the reception of these charisms (given for the exercise of the apostolate), even the ordinary ones, there arises for every one of the faithful the right and duty to exercise them in the church and in the world for the good of humanity and for the building up of the church. They do this in the freedom of the Spirit who "blows where he wills" (Jn 3, 8) and, at the same time, in communion with the fellowship in Christ. (*AA* 3)

This freedom to exercise the gifts of the Holy Spirit must be respected within the churches, even if it has not yet been given clear canonical recognition.

In addition to these stated rights of individual members of the church, the *local communities* of the Christian faithful also have rights which command respect. Some are mentioned explicitly or obliquely in the codes, while others are derived from the canons[19] or inferred from the nature of local churches:

a) *Existence.* Local communities which are established as parishes are "juridic persons," that is, they are recognized and have standing in Canon Law as permanent entities. They have a right to remain in existence. This means that they cannot be suppressed or merged unless it is demonstrated that they are no longer viable as communities of the Christian faithful.

b) *Maintain Communion.* Parishes and other local Catholic congregations are obliged to maintain the bonds of communion: faith, sacraments, and governance. In return, they have rights of communion: reciprocity, assistance, and support from the diocese and other local churches.

c) *Equality.* Catholic communities differ from each other in many ways, for example, size, age, wealth, ethnic composition, rural or urban setting, and so on. But they possess a fundamental equality and dignity as congregations of the faithful, true local churches in which Christ is present and in which the Holy Spirit dwells.

d) *Word and Sacraments.* God's holy people are nourished by God's word and the sacraments. Their right to the preaching of the word and the celebration of the sacraments is both basic and communal. The right of local congregations to the Eucharist is the preeminent instance of this more general right.

e) *Pastoral Leadership and Ministry.* Communities of believers have a right to a pastor or other pastoral leader to reside with them, know them, support and assist them. Pastoral ministers provide guidance and organization within the community as well as preaching, catechesis, and sacramental preparation.

f) *Activities and Services.* Congregations have the right to express their faith in pastoral initiatives, apostolic actions, projects for justice, and works of charity. They find their own ways to promote social justice and assist the poor in their locale and across the world.

g) *Information, Communication, Consultation.* Parish communities have a right to accurate and timely information about matters which affect them, and to effective consultation which affords opportunities for the expression of their needs, desires, and opinions.

h) *Formation and Education.* Local churches have the right as well as the duty to form their members in the faith. This includes the preparation of new members for initiation, the education of children and youths, and the ongoing formation for adults.

i) *Evangelization and Mission.* The church is missionary by its very nature, and each local church shares in the duty and right to foster and further that missionary activity. All Catholic communities participate in proclaiming and witnessing to Christ's message of salvation.

j) *Spiritual Growth.* Each parish must attend to its own spiritual health and welfare. It has the obligation and right to pursue its own repentance, conversion, and spiritual development. The local church needs ongoing reform and sanctification, and it has the right to choose the ways to achieve these ends.

k) *Goods and Property.* Parishes and other juridic persons have the right to acquire, use, administer, and dispose of their own goods and property. Local congregations possess a legitimate autonomy and responsibility for their buildings, furnishings, and funds.

l) *Vindication and Defense of Rights.* Communities of the faithful have the same rights and obligations to claim their prerogatives and defend themselves against offenses that individual Catholics do. Parishes have standing as juridic persons, and other stable, non-parochial local communities of the faithful should be accorded it.

The church is essentially a communion of communions. This means that the rights and freedoms of its primary components, namely local congregations, must be taken seriously and respected. For both communities and individuals within them, these canonical rights serve as markers or boundaries of their legitimate freedoms. Their importance in the ministry of canonists is obvious.

INCULTURATION

The Catholic communion's identity as a world church became increasingly clear during the final quarter of the twentieth century. A "world church" is not simply global or "universal" in extension, that is, spread over or represented in all parts of the world. A world church is one which is inculturated in all areas of the globe, one engaged in honest and earnest dialogue with the diverse cultures of the world. A world church is consciously and reciprocally influencing and being influenced by those cultures.

In other terms, the "catholicity" of the church means more than a numerical or symbolic presence around the whole world, it also implies an active and mutual engagement with all of the cultures encountered by the communion of churches.

The church's vigorous missionary efforts in the sixteenth century could be characterized as an international spread of a European expression of Catholic Christianity. Today Catholicism is no longer a "European religious export" to the rest of the world, but a faith tradition that is taking root among indigenous peoples, races, and societies of all kinds. The church is a communion of truly local communities, at home in their surroundings, no longer an exotic transplant from a foreign culture.

Inculturation is impossible without freedom and flexibility. Uniformity of expression and practice stands in the way of effective inculturation. The need for local churches to take root and grow "in native soil" requires a large freedom to adapt both the articulation of the faith and the discipline of its practice.

A conviction about the need for genuine inculturation (which is also termed "contextualization") of the churches was born in the theology of mission, and matured into general acceptance in a series of papal and synodal documents.

Pope Paul VI wrote about the concept in his 1975 exhortation on evangelization: "The individual churches...have the task of assimilating the essence of the gospel message and of transposing it...into the language that these particular people understand, then of proclaiming it in this language."[20] Paul VI used the word "language" here in an anthropological and cultural sense, and he added that the "transpositions" are to take place in the areas of liturgical expression, catechesis, theological formulation, ecclesial structures, and ministry.[21]

The Episcopal Synod of 1985 defined the notion of inculturation as it is currently understood within the church:

> [Inculturation] means the intimate transformation of authentic cultural values through their integration in Christianity and the insertion of Christianity in the various human cultures.[22]

Pope John Paul II has spoken of inculturation on many occasions. One major discussion was in his 1990 encyclical on missionary activity:

> Through inculturation the church makes the Gospel incarnate in different cultures and at the same time introduces peoples, together with their cultures, into her own community. She transmits to them her own values, at the same time taking the good elements which already exist in them and renewing them from within. Through inculturation the church, for her part, becomes a more intelligible sign of what she is and a more effective instrument of mission.[23]

In the encyclical the pope envisions inculturation as an action of the local churches affecting various sectors of Christian life such as evangelization, worship, theology, charitable works, and church renewal. Obviously the entire process of inculturation implies and demands a substantial zone of freedom in which to make these necessary adaptations.

Recognition of the need for inculturation reached a high level in the 1998 Episcopal Synod for Asia, which called for the churches rooted in Asia to grow more Asian in appearance so that they did not look like churches foreign to Asia's traditions and cultures.[24] Inculturation was viewed by the bishops of Asia as "a major missionary challenge" for the church.[25] They seek churches with "Asian faces and voices."

Inculturation has broad ramifications. It affects modes of evangelization, catechetical approaches, liturgical celebrations, spiritualities and prayer forms, interreligious dialogues, theological expressions, community discipline (e.g., selection of bishops, synodal decision-making), and pastoral care. Genuine inculturation presupposes the freedom for the churches to make needed modifications in all these areas.

CHURCHES AS VOLUNTARY ASSOCIATIONS

Finally, there is the underlying social reality that in nearly all countries today churches are voluntary associations. People are relatively free to join them or to walk away from them, to be actively engaged in them or nominally identified with them. This freedom of association is an undeniable fact of life, and it qualifies and conditions all disciplinary activity, including the canonical, within the churches.

Voluntary choice governs church involvement both 1) at the level of ecclesial membership, ongoing affiliation, and personal identification, and 2) at the level of local church loyalty, Mass attendance, active participation, and financial support.

Membership, Affiliation, Identification

Membership in a church is unlike belonging to a family, being married, holding citizenship, or serving in the military. Once born into a family, one can never leave it, although it is possible to be excluded or "disowned." Marriage is a voluntary contract, but one is not free to simply withdraw from it. Marriage is enforced and supported by the law; divorce requires a civil proce-dure. Citizenship is awarded at birth or by naturalization, and it is not an easy matter to change. Some legal action is required. And military service, even when entered by voluntary enlistment rather than by conscription, cannot be left at will. One must serve out one's time before being discharged.

All of these affiliations enjoy the favor of the civil law. They are supported by some level of legal sanction. That is not true of church membership. Indeed, in some religiously dominated or secular states there are negative sanctions attached to member-ship in a Christian church.

In some places there are strong social and traditional sup-ports for Catholic churches. Nearly everyone is identified as Catholic, and it is the ordinary expectation for people to belong. In addition, there are very often regional, ethnic, and family ties to the Catholic Church which are very powerful and go back hun-dreds of years. These connections with the church are frequently reinforced by convictions of faith and a sense of moral obliga-tion. In other nations where religious pluralism or religious indifference predominate, Catholics sometimes change affilia-tion more readily, for example, when entering a mixed marriage or remarrying after divorce.

To insist that religious affiliation is voluntary is not to imply that it is a choice made in absolute freedom apart from all influ-ences or predispositions. Obviously the choices are heavily weighted by moral values, faith convictions, personal and social circumstances. Still, at various points in people's lives, church identification is an option that is maintained or altered by per-sonal decision.

Loyalty to and Participation in a Local Church

Engagement with the local Catholic congregation, espe-cially in fluid and mobile societies, is even more a matter of per-sonal and family choice. Sociologists distinguish parishioners as nuclear (most active), modal (ordinary members), marginal (rarely involved), or dormant (inactive). In urban areas especially, it is easy to attend parishes other than one's own, where liturgies and homilies are more to one's liking, or to lapse into relative inactivity.

Long-time parishioners at St. Mary's on Main Street remember losing a lot of members when they had to close their school, and when the neighboring parish air-conditioned its church. But they also saw their numbers increase when they started an RCIA program, and breathed new life into their liturgical celebrations and their religious education program.

In many parts of the world, there are millions of nominal Catholics who maintain virtually no affiliation with or participation in the local church. Many bring their children to be baptized and ask for church burial, but have little to do with the church otherwise.

This brief comment on the voluntary nature of church affiliation and participation is not intended as a value judgment, good or bad. It simply points out a very real social condition within which all church rules are made and applied. It is not a confined and coercive context, as within the military or even like national citizenship, rather it is a voluntary one in which personal motivations and options are decisive.

In Conclusion

These several parameters of Christian freedom mark the boundaries of the mighty composite of freedom within the church. This "protected zone of freedom" is like a cherished homeland to be defended and promoted.

The Second Vatican Council clearly enunciated this freedom within the church:

> All in the church must preserve unity in essentials (in necesariis). But let all, according to the gifts which they have received, maintain a proper freedom (debitam libertatem servent) in their various forms of spiritual life and discipline, in

their different liturgical rites, and even in their theological elaborations of revealed truth. In all things let charity *(caritatem)* prevail. *(UR* 4)[26]

In essentials, unity; in doubtful matters, freedom; in all things, charity. Freedom, like unity and charity, is a theological imperative. It must be a foremost concern of canonical ministry in the church.

CHAPTER 6

GOOD ORDER IN THE CHURCH:

SECOND FOCUS OF THE

CANONICAL MINISTRY

Make sure that everything is done properly and in good order...since God is a God, not of confusion, but of peace. (1 Cor 14, 40, 33)

THE MINISTRY OF CANONISTS must focus on freedom, but it must also be concerned about good order within the churches. The canonist is to maintain ample space for the initiatives and "breathing" of the Holy Spirit,[1] and at the same time ensure orderly and fair procedures.

This chapter addresses the nature of and the need for authority in the churches so that both good order and freedom will thrive. It is important to recall and reexamine the origin and character of authority within the Christian tradition. Authority is not an alien concept, even within communities of love. Indeed, after instructing the Corinthians in the value of spiritual gifts, the Apostle Paul exhorted them to do everything "properly and in good order" in their assemblies.[2]

The chapter unfolds along these lines: 1) the language of power in Canon Law, 2) the sources of power in the New Testament, 3) the scope of Christ's authority, 4) Jesus' teaching about authority as service, 5) some historical distortions of the exercise of authority, 6) the teaching of the Second Vatican Council on authority, 7) the concept and reality of "hierarchy," 8) authority in the churches as participative, and 9) laity and the power of governance.

POWER LANGUAGE IN CANON LAW

Canon Law is laden with the language of power. The word "power" *(potestas)* occurs more than two hundred times in the 1983 *Code of Canon Law,* and about the same number of times in the 1990 *Code of Canons of the Eastern Churches.* The word "authority" *(auctoritas)* is used nearly three hundred times in the 1983 *Code.* By contrast, God is mentioned by name only sixty-one times. Other power terms like "jurisdiction," "faculty," "mandate," "office," and "duty" are also frequently employed in the canons. Canonical commentators carefully distinguish the shades of meaning in these terms.

The heavy use of power language should come as no surprise. After all, Canon Law, as a system of rules, is largely concerned with the assignment of responsibilities within the church. Many of the canons specify duties: who has the obligation to do what. Consequently, persons are endowed with the authority or power to carry out their responsibilities. For example, presbyters have the faculty to preach the word of God everywhere (c. 764), since they are bound to proclaim the gospel (c. 757).

The use of authority language is expected, even inevitable, in any set of rules. What might be unexpected is the style and kind of authority language encountered in Roman Catholic Canon Law, because it was drawn more extensively from its Roman law sources than from the terminology and imagery of the New Testament, the church's own "charter document."

SOURCES OF POWER IN THE NEW TESTAMENT

In every religion or religious movement, God is believed to be the source of power. The persons who bear God's revelation give testimony of their proximity to or contact with God. In the Judeo-Christian tradition God is often referred to in power terms, as the "All-Powerful" or "Almighty."

In the New Testament the sources of power derived from God are manifested historically through Jesus Christ and through the Holy Spirit. For Christians, Jesus was the ultimate revelation of God, in fact, he was God-become-human for the salvation of the world. After his crucifixion and death, Jesus was raised from the dead and made known to his disciples as "Lord," and the Risen Christ is acknowledged to be the source of all authority in the church.

New Testament Greek uses two different power words, *exousia,* meaning power, liberty, authority, or government, and *dunamis,* meaning power, ability, capacity, or force. Their shades of meaning are close, and their usage is almost interchangeable.

Christ's power is described in these terms:

All power *(exousia)* on heaven and on earth has been given to me. (Mt 28, 18)

The message of the cross is foolishness to those who are perishing, but to us who are being saved it is the power *(dunamis)* of God....Christ is the power *(dunamis)* of God. (1 Cor 1, 18 and 24)

All power and authority in the church is derived from Christ the Lord, but it is made active and operative in the life of the church through the Holy Spirit. After Jesus was taken up to heaven, there was a sort of transition of authority, "a transfer of power." The Spirit whom Jesus had repeatedly promised was sent down upon his disciples.

You will receive power *(dunamis)* when the Holy Spirit comes upon you, and you will be my witnesses in Jerusalem, throughout Judea and Samaria, and to the ends of the earth. (Acts 1, 8)

When the time for Pentecost was fulfilled, they were all in one place together. And suddenly there came from the sky a noise like a driving wind, and it filled the entire house where they were. Then there appeared to them tongues as of fire, which parted and came to rest on each one of them. And they were all filled with the Holy Spirit and began to speak in different tongues, as the Spirit enabled them to proclaim. (Acts 2, 1–4)

[Peter proclaimed] God raised this Jesus; of this we are all witnesses. Exalted at the right hand of God, he received the promise of the Holy Spirit from the Father and poured it forth as you both see and hear. (Acts 2, 33–34)

This Holy Spirit, sent from the Father, empowered that earliest community of Christ's followers, and has continued to empower the expanding mission of the churches ever since.

THE SCOPE OF CHRIST'S AUTHORITY

Jesus of Nazareth was anointed by God with the Holy Spirit and power (*dunamis;* Acts 10, 38). He was conceived through the action of the Holy Spirit and the overshadowing power of the Most High (Lk 1, 35). He was the conveyor of power which went out from him (Lk 8, 46) and healed large numbers of people (Lk 6, 19). His miracles or "mighty deeds" *(dunameis)* were acts of power.

Jesus the Nazarean was a man whom God sent to you with miracles, wonders, and signs as his credentials. These God worked through him in your midst, as you well know. (Acts 2, 22)

Jesus, during his life, described and demonstrated the scope of his authority in many ways. His Father had given him authority *(exousia)* over all people, so that he could give eternal life to them (Jn 17, 1–2). To those who accepted him, he gave power to become children of God (Jn 1, 12). The Father gave him power to exercise judgment, because he was the Son of Man (Jn 5, 27). He had power to forgive sins, and healed a paralytic to prove it (Mk 2, 10–11). He was perceived to teach with authority (Mk 1, 22 and 27), like a prophet.

Jesus gave power and authority *(dunamis kai exousia)* to the Twelve (and to the seventy-two; Lk 10, 1ff.) to cast out demons and to cure diseases (Lk 9, 1; Mk 3, 15), and the disciples rejoiced at their successful use of it (Lk 10, 17–19). At his departure he sent the Holy Spirit upon his disciples, and they were clothed with power *(dunamis)* from on high (Lk 24, 49). The apostles bore witness to his resurrection with great power *(dunamis;* Acts 4, 33).

The authority *(exousia)* given to the Apostle Paul was given to build up the Christian community and its members (2 Cor 10, 8; 13, 10). He led the Gentiles to Christ "by the power of signs and wonders, by the power of the Spirit" (Rom 15, 19). He preached the gospel "in power and in the Holy Spirit" (1 Thes 1, 5). The power of Christ was present to the apostle in the Spirit.

The faith of the community rested on the power *(dunamis)* of God, not on words of wisdom, after Paul had shown them God's mystery in spirit and power (1 Cor 2, 4–5). The community of believers drew its strength from the Lord and from his mighty power (Eph 6, 10). The community itself had power or freedom with regard to its own observance, for example, in regard to eating meat which had been sacrificed to idols (1 Cor 8, 9; 10, 23). The power of the Holy Spirit caused the church to abound in hope (Rom 15, 13). The Spirit strengthened the local church with power, so that they could comprehend the full dimensions of Christ's love for them (Eph 3, 14–19). The community also shared in the powerful gift of the Spirit, "mighty deeds" (1 Cor 12, 10 and 28).

Three distinctive characteristics of the powerful actions of Christ, as witnessed in the New Testament, deserve special mention here:

1) Jesus worked his miracles in the context of faith. These acts of power presupposed the faith of both the one acting and the one acted upon. He did not work mighty deeds in Nazareth because their faith was lacking (Mt 13, 58), and he cured the boy possessed with a mute spirit only after faith was evoked (Mk 9, 14ff.).

2) The miracles occurred in human history. They are the eternal rule of God breaking into the present moment

(Mt 12, 28), foreshadowing and signaling to humanity God's saving purpose for the world.

3) The powerful works of Christ were saving acts. They demonstrate the power of God for the deliverance of humankind. Only God can save, and the power *(dunamis)* of God is for the salvation of everyone who believes (Mt 19, 26; Rom 1, 16).

AUTHORITY AS SERVICE

The distinctively Christian exercise of authority is of supreme importance for the purpose of this present writing. This unique dimension of authority as service is sometimes described as simply a matter of style, a recommended way of exercising authority in the church. On the contrary, authority as service goes to the very essence of what power is within the church. It reveals the nature of Christ's mission.

Few themes stand out as clearly and forcefully in the New Testament. Parallel passages in all four gospels point to an authentic saying of Jesus, remembered and repeated by all the evangelists for the benefit of their own communities, the people and their leaders.

In Mark and Matthew the saying on authority is placed after the bold request by the brothers James and John for places of special favor at Jesus' right and left sides in his future kingdom. Jesus responded that the positions were not his to give, but when the other ten (of the Twelve) heard of the brothers' request, they became indignant.

> Jesus summoned them and said to them, "You know that those who are recognized as rulers of the Gentiles lord it over them, and their great ones make their authority over them felt. But it shall not be so among you. Rather, whoever wishes to be great among you will be your servant; whoever wishes to be first among you will be the slave of all. For the Son of Man did not come to be served but to serve, and to give his life as a ransom for many."[3]

The language is strong. "Lord it over them" and "make their authority felt" vividly express the exercise of raw power by Roman imperial rulers, the occupying force in Israel at the time. "Servant" *(diakonos)* means "one who waits on tables," and "slave" *(doulos)* is "one in bondage to another," quite literally in servitude. These are humble roles indeed.

The message is clear: authority in Christian communities is like Jesus' own life of service. It means being at the service of others, pure and simple. There is no self-aggrandizement, no ambitious striving for higher or more prestigious positions, no domination of others. Power in the church of Christ is power to serve.

The parallel passages in Luke and John are narrated in the context of the Last Supper:

> Then an argument broke out among them about which of them should be regarded as the greatest. He said to them, "The kings of the Gentiles lord it over them, and those in authority over them are addressed as 'Benefactors'; but among you it shall not be so. Rather, let the greatest among you be as the youngest, and the leaders as the servant. For who is greater: the one seated at the table or the one who serves? Is it not the one seated at the table? I am among you as the one who serves." (Lk 22, 24–27)

Jesus' own sense of impending death and his personal servant-like actions add dramatic power to John's narrative:

> So, during supper, fully aware that the Father had put everything into his power, and that he had come from God and was returning to God, he rose from the meal and took off his outer garments. He took a towel and tied it around his waist. Then he poured water into a basin and began to wash the disciples' feet and dry them with the towel around his waist....So when he had washed their feet [and] put his garments back on and reclined at table again, he said to them, "Do you realize what I have done for you? You call me 'teacher' and 'master,' and rightly so, for indeed I am. If I, therefore, the master and teacher, have washed your feet, you ought to wash one another's feet. I have given you a

model to follow, so that as I have done for you, you should also do." (Jn 13, 2–15)

This same strong theme of authority as service is also clearly affirmed in Mark 9, 35, "If anyone wishes to be first, he shall be the last of all and the servant of all," and 1 Peter 5, 3, "Do not lord it over those who are assigned to you, but be examples to the flock."

This powerful gospel teaching is no mere passing remark or situational observation, which might have been occasioned by leadership conflicts within the early communities. Rather, this teaching on authority as service is rooted in the very identity and mission of Jesus Christ. Jesus viewed his own role as one of service, an unstinting service that extended even to his freely willed death. He was a servant to his people and to God's reign, both in life and in death. The norm of servanthood[4] as authority is authentic, bedrock Christianity. It defines the very nature of authority in the church, not simply the mode or style of its exercise.

The Apostle Paul described himself in the same terms: Who is Paul? The minister *(diakonos)* through whom you became believers (1 Cor 3, 5). His was a "ministry *(diakonia)* of the Spirit" which brought salvation, and was both life-giving and liberating (2 Cor 3, 6 and 17). His was a "ministry of reconciliation," not only within the Christian community, but of God's reconciliation of the world to himself in Christ (2 Cor 5, 18–19).

Paul's ministry was one of complex involvement with local communities of Christians: preaching, teaching, and giving them a personal example, so that they might mature into "spiritual people."[5] He tried to help them become responsible and well-ordered communities, within which individuals used their gifts for the common good (1 Cor 12, 7). "Everything should be done for building up" (1 Cor 14, 26). Although Paul sometimes spoke in authoritarian tones (e.g., 1 Cor 5 and 6), he was not a self-promoter. He labored, strained, and suffered in order to *serve* his communities.

This authentic notion of authority as service has often been distorted in the church through the course of history. Many of these mutations, borrowings from secular counterparts, seemed necessary and appropriate at the time they took place. And many of these disfigurations might be considered inevitable, since the church is, after all, only a flawed band of sinful people. But cumulatively they have altered the nature and use of authority in the church.

DISTORTIONS OF AUTHORITY

Historical developments have shaped and reshaped the church's authority as the heat and pressure of the molding process bends and reshapes laminated wood. Many of these changes though gradual were of long duration. These transforming circumstances are well known, scholars have examined them thoroughly, and they are recorded in historical studies of the church.[6] Here it will suffice to mention a few of them, in order to call to mind some of the trends and forces which caused changes in the way that church authority was exercised and perceived.

1. The very growth and spread of the Christian movement complicated its life and caused changes in its internal relationships. In the third and fourth centuries the number of local churches multiplied, spreading out from the cities into villages and countrysides, and taking root in diverse cultural settings around the Mediterranean basin. From small, contained communities wherein everyone knew everyone else, the churches evolved into clusters of communities, founded from and dependent upon a "mother church." Presbyters were often sent out from an urban center to country parishes, instead of being chosen from within the local community. The bishop became a superintendent of all the churches of the area, rather than the pastor of a single community. Thus the personal connection between the community and its ministers began to change as a result of this early growth.

2. The roles of service within communities, once many and diverse (e.g., the many different functions described in the New Testament or those symbolically represented by the four minor and three major orders), in the fourth century began to be

absorbed into the single office of the presbyter. He gradually became the *factotum*, the one really active person in the liturgical assembly and in the pastoral activity of the congregation. Everyone else regressed to the status of passive observer or recipient of ministry.

3. In the beginning Christianity fought to survive as a minority sect within the Roman Empire, and sometimes the church was viciously persecuted. After the Peace of Constantine, however, it had to adjust to the official embrace accorded it as an established church. Bishops became officials of the Roman rule, honored but also weighed down with duties having little to do with the preaching of the gospel. Some were charged with organizing the defense of their cities or judging civil disputes. For instance, Augustine, while bishop of Hippo, spent many hours each day settling civil conflicts over properties and inheritances. This new status altered the bishops' relationship to their people and to the government, and it blurred the true nature and scope of their authority.

4. Christianity was born into a world controlled by the Roman Empire, and was inevitably influenced by its laws and customs. Roman law had, and still has, an immense and pervasive influence on the exercise of authority within the church. In the early centuries church leaders freely borrowed concepts and procedures from the legal system of the empire. Christian emperors[7] themselves passed many laws governing church activities. In addition to the many terms, notions, and offices borrowed directly from the Roman system,[8] the mentality and attitude of the Roman civil jurists consistently colored the church's own internal relationships. One result of the influence of Roman law is a juridicized mode of administration, the tendency to treat issues in legal rather than in moral or pastoral categories. For example, the church still deals with the problem of divorce and remarriage by means of a legal determination of the status of persons, that is, whether the person is still married or free to marry. In short, it would be difficult to overestimate the influence that Roman law has had on Canon Law.

5. In contrast to the influence of Roman law, it was Germanic property law which propelled the spread of "proprietary

churches" in the early Middle Ages. The owners of rural properties often built, endowed, and maintained local churches on their
own land. The church, rectory, cemetery, fields, stole fees, and
tithes all belonged to the landlord. He appointed the priest,
often from among his serfs, and could control or remove him.
The landlord was entitled to a share of the parish income. This
system of proprietary churches became deeply ingrained in
medieval culture, so that church authorities had to strive might-
ily to reassert the bishop's supervisory control over the priests
and the private churches.

6. The proprietary churches contributed to the development of the ecclesiastical benefice system in the ninth and tenth
centuries. A benefice is a sacred office, like that of pastor or
bishop, to which is connected the right to receive the income
from the endowment attached to the office. It was a church
office with a reliable source of income for the officeholder. In
time income became the central focus, and, by means of dispensations, individual clerics were able to hold multiple benefices.
That is, they accumulated "pluralities" of offices, collected the
incomes from them, and hired someone else to perform the pastoral duties. Sometimes they never even visited the churches in
which they held the leading office. Although these abuses were
eventually extirpated after the Council of Trent, the benefice system endured well into the twentieth century.

7. The church's confrontations with civil governmental
authority have affected its own claims and uses of authority. The
struggle in the eleventh and twelfth centuries to free the church
from domination by secular powers, epitomized by the "lay
investiture controversy"[9] was a case in point. It caused Pope Gregory VII to assert (in 1075) that the pope has the power to depose
emperors as well as bishops, and that he himself may be judged
by no one. In a similar vein, Pope Boniface VIII claimed (in
1302) the supremacy of the church's spiritual authority over any
and all temporal powers, and declared that it is necessary for salvation that every human creature be subject to the Roman pontiff. These exaggerated claims were viewed as necessary in the
battle to wrest the power of appointments to church offices from

the kings and princes and return them to the church's own authority.

8. The Protestant Reformation and the Catholic reaction to it caused still other assertions of church authority which were not entirely free of exaggeration. For example, at the Council of Trent (1545–63) bishops were often characterized as delegates of the pope in matters of church reform rather than acting with their own episcopal authority within their churches. This strategy was seen as a way of "strengthening their hand" against local secular powers, but it also contributed to the enlargement of papal power and the diminution of the rightful authority of bishops.

9. The canonical restriction which provided that only clerics may obtain the power of jurisdiction or occupy church offices[10] solidified the control of all ministry by the ordained. These restrictive measures were often prompted by efforts to reform corrupt practices related to church offices or to fend off the incursions of secular authorities that attempted to exercise power within the church. Yet they also served to impede and discourage active lay involvement in the life and ministry of the churches.

10. Surely the greatest single distortion of authority in the history of the church is the evolution of the papacy into an absolute monarchy. In virtue of the Lord's selection of Peter as first among the apostles, the bishop of the Church of Rome now claims supreme, full, immediate, and universal power in the church, which he can always freely exercise, as well as power over all particular churches and groupings of churches. In other terms, the pope possesses the fullness of executive, legislative, and judicial power in the church, with no separation powers, no "checks and balances." There is no recourse or appeal from his decisions or decrees. The pope is joined together with all of the bishops in one college, but he has the right to act personally rather than collegially, and he often does.[11]

These historical events and trends briefly illustrate the uses of church authority in very diverse circumstances, and they give some perspective on the exercise of ecclesiastical power within the vicissitudes of history. But such historical developments must be recognized as contingent compromises and temporary strategies. They must not be viewed as necessary attributes of the church, given by Christ or willed by God as permanent fixtures. When recognized as historical developments, they can be reexamined and measured against the teachings of Christ, the content of the gospels, and the apostolic tradition. Then decisions can be made as to their continued usefulness.

The distortions of authority might be compared to an overgrown garden. The whole appearance of the place is changed by growth out of control. Its beauty and original plan are so obscured that it looks like only a field of weeds, and no longer like a cherished garden.

THE SECOND VATICAN COUNCIL ON AUTHORITY

The Council, in its teaching on church authority, attempted to correct some of the distortions caused by historical events and turnings. Vatican II went a long way toward restoring the original biblical vision of authority as service. In its central and most solemn document the Council said:

> For the nourishment and continual growth of the people of God, Christ the Lord instituted a variety of ministries which are directed towards the good of the whole body. Ministers who are endowed with sacred power are at the service of their brothers and sisters, so that all who belong to the people of God, and therefore enjoy real Christian dignity, by cooperating with each other freely and in an orderly manner in pursuit of the same goal, may attain salvation. (*LG* 18)

> The bishops, therefore, have undertaken along with their fellow workers, the priests and deacons, the service of the community. (*LG* 20)

> This [episcopal] office which the Lord entrusted to the shepherds of his people is a true service, and in holy scripture it is significantly called "diaconia" or ministry. (*LG* 24)[12]

> The bishops govern the churches entrusted to them as vicars and legates of Christ, by counsel, persuasion and example

and indeed also by authority and sacred power which they make use of only to build up their flock in truth and holiness, remembering that the greater must become as the younger and the leader as one who serves.[13]

In summary, the teaching of the Council on authority as service is strong and clear:

1) the communities of God's people stand in first place, as those to be served, followed in the second position by those who serve; that is to say, the communities have priority over those who minister within them;
2) the ministers, after the pattern of Christ himself, are in service to their communities;
3) the mode of service is to be collaborative and cooperative, making use of counsel, persuasion, and example, as well as sacred power;
4) and the purpose of it all, the common goal, beyond the building up of the churches, is the salvation of the world.

Thus the Council restored and reoriented the notion of what authority means within the church. It revived the authentic concept of authority as service as over against a secular, governmental, or military sense of authority.

The Gospel of Matthew offers dramatic examples of these contrasting systems of authority: when the Roman centurion in Capernaum asked Jesus to cure his paralyzed servant, he declared,

> I too am a person subject to authority, with soldiers subject to me. And I say to one, "Go," and he goes; and to another, "Come here,"' and he comes; and to my slave, "Do this," and he does it. (Mt 8, 9)

However, Jesus instructed his own disciples quite differently:

> But it shall not be so among you. Rather whoever wishes to be great among you shall be your servant, whoever wishes to be first among you shall be your slave. Just so, the Son of

Man did not come to be served, but to serve. (Mt 20, 26–27)

Pope John Paul II singled out the doctrine of "hierarchical authority as service" (from chapter 3 of *LG*) as one of the "elements which characterize the true and genuine image of the church," one of the things which "constitute the substantial *newness* of the Second Vatican Council" and "constitute likewise the *newness* of the new Code."[14]

HIERARCHY: CONCEPT AND REALITY

It is hard to imagine a descriptive term less congenial to the authentic sense of authority as service than the word "hierarchy." Hierarchy describes a system of persons ranked in grades or classes, one above another, the governance of a subservient group by an elite group. It conveys a meaning of rulers and ruled, a sense of "those who make their authority felt" over others. It implies quite the opposite of being "servants of all" or of one who "did not come to be served but to serve." Etymologically hierarchy means simply "priestly rule" or "sacred authority."[15]

How the Christian church came to use such an unseemly term for its leadership group is both a fascinating story and a tragic mistake. For "hierarchy" is not a biblical expression; it is not found in the scriptures at all. It was not even a term used in ordinary Greek at the time the Christian churches were formed. The word was literally invented by Dionysius, the Pseudo-Areopagite, and was accepted and widely used because of his exaggerated prominence.

Dionysius the (real) Areopagite was one of those who became believers after hearing the Apostle Paul preach in the Areopagus (a promontory near the Acropolis) of Athens in about the year 50, the middle of the first century.

> At that point, Paul left them. A few did join him, however, to become believers. Among these were Dioynsius, a member of the court of the Areopagus, a woman named Damaris, and a few others. (Acts 17, 34)

This Dionysius, according to the historian Eusebius, later became the first bishop of Athens.[16]

Much later, in late fifth or early sixth century (perhaps between 465 and 490) a Christian mystic and Neoplatonic philosopher wrote four theological treatises and ten letters. The author claimed to be Dionysius the Areopagite. He said that he witnessed the eclipse of the sun at the time of Jesus' crucifixion, that he was with St. Peter and St. James at the death of the Blessed Virgin, and that Paul was his teacher. His claims were believed: the fifth-century writer was mistakenly thought to be who he claimed to be, the first-century disciple of the Apostle Paul.

For a thousand years this pretender was assumed to be the Pauline convert, disciple, and witness. Consequently his writings were accorded very great respect and had immense influence, perhaps greater than any of the fathers of the church, and just a little less than the books of the scriptures themselves. Pope Gregory the Great (590–605) cited Dionysius, and Pope Martin I relied on his writings at the Lateran Council of 649. The thirteenth-century scholastic theologians studied and quoted his works. For example, Thomas Aquinas cited Dionysius seventeen hundred times!

It was not until the fifteenth and sixteenth centuries that the authorship of the works of this "Dionysius" began to be seriously questioned, and it was not until the end of the nineteenth century that they were conclusively proven to have been written much later than the first century. The identity of the true author still remains a mystery.

One of the treatises of Pseudo-Dionysius is entitled *The Celestial Hierarchy.*[17] In it the author describes the descending orders of the angels, closer to or more distant from God. This is the source for the traditional "nine choirs" of angels. In another work, *The Ecclesiastical Hierarchy,*[18] Pseudo-Dionysius created an order and function of the church's ministers parallel to that of the angels in heaven. First his notion of hierarchy, then its application within the church:

> In my opinion a hierarchy is a sacred order, a state of understanding and an activity approximating as closely as possible to

the divine. And it is uplifted to the imitation of God in proportion to the enlightenments divinely given to it. (*CH* 3)

If you talk of "hierarchy" you are referring in effect to the arrangement of all the sacred realities. Talk of "hierarch" and one is referring to a holy and inspired man, someone who understands all sacred knowledge, someone in whom an entire hierarchy is completely perfected and known. (*EH* 1.3)

Pseudo-Dionysius envisioned a spiritual universe, along the lines of Plato's philosophy, in which divine illumination descended to creatures and they ascended toward divinization through hierarchical mediation. Hierarchy denoted a subordination within which the sacred superiors related to inferiors in such a way that the lower orders were gradually raised up to God by their superiors. In the church power was transmitted through enlightened intermediaries.

This is the remarkable origin of the term "hierarchy." Without denying the philosophical symmetry or even the spiritual beauty of Pseudo-Dionysius' vision, it can be asserted that it bears little resemblance to reality, either the reality of how authority functions in actual churches "on the ground," for example, at St. Mary's on Main Street (even when the bishop comes to visit!), or the reality of Jesus' teaching in the gospels about authority as service.

The expression "hierarchy" *(hierarchia)* does not appear in the 1983 *Code of Canon Law.* Its adjectival form "hierarchical" *(hierachicus, a, um)* is used only nine times.[19] This most unfortunate term, of such curiously mistaken origin, is passing into desuetude in canonical usage, and should be headed toward oblivion in the church.

AUTHORITY AS PARTICIPATIVE

Authority in the churches is necessarily participative. The necessity arises from the nature of the church as a communion of the faithful, and as a people who are fundamentally equal.[20] Those who belong to this people have the right and duty to be actively engaged in the direction of the church, just as all are to be active participants in its actions of worship.

Every person is fully incorporated into a local church through baptism, confirmation, and the most holy Eucharist. All receive forgiveness of sins and a new life of grace. All enjoy the indwelling of the Holy Spirit and share the Spirit's gifts. All cooperate in the exercise of the priestly office of Jesus Christ.[21]

From the very beginning not all of God's people have taken part in the leadership of the churches in the same way. Each one has different talents, callings, training, aptitudes, and circumstances. Some have studied long and hard in preparation for their ministries of leadership, while others have rich experience or keen intellect. Yet everyone has a role to play in serving the church.

The oldest and most authentic form of the exercise of authority among the churches is conciliar or synodal. From the time of the "Council of Jerusalem" (Acts 15) on, the synodal instinct and practice has endured among the churches. Local and regional meetings of representatives of the churches, recorded in the early centuries of Christianity, were the accepted and preferred occasions for decision-making and policy-forming. Patriarchal and metropolitan synods were a regular part of the life of the churches. Ecumenical councils became the major events for reform and renewal within the church universal.

"Conciliarity" or "synodality" visibly expresses the nature of the church as a communion of communities. These terms describe the context within which individual church authorities (i.e., the pope, bishops, pastors) function. They also provide the paradigm for leadership within the local church, for example, diocesan and parish pastoral councils.

These conciliar structures do not stand over against individual ministers within the churches. There is no opposition between them. Rather the councils (parish, diocesan) are collaborative counterparts, sources of the Spirit's wisdom, and represent the collective voice of God's people. The Spirit guides the churches by means of creative, and sometimes tensive, interaction between these two embodiments of authority, that is, members and ministers joined "in council" with one another.

"Collegiality" is the name given to the shared authority of all of the bishops of the world together with the bishop of Rome. But authority is shared at all other levels of the church's existence as well. The pastor and the parishioners at St. Mary's on Main Street work together (both within and outside the parish council) to lead the local community, which is the primary reality of church. Particular churches or dioceses receive direction from the bishop together with the priests, deacons, religious, and laypersons who consult with him. Episcopal conferences give guidance to the churches of nations or regions in a similarly participative way.

Participation in the exercise of church authority takes various forms and modes. There are deliberative bodies which require formal sharing in their decision-making processes, for example, bishops voting in an ecumenical council or a patriarchal synod or episcopal conference, or presbyters in a college of consultors, or religious in a chapter or council. The co-responsibility of the voting members for the decisions taken in such bodies is clear and measurable—the votes are counted.

More often participation in authority structures is of a consultative nature. In the canonical tradition consultation is an authentic expression of the community's proper role in the exercise of authority. It represents a serious and weighty engagement in policy-making and decisions, especially in local churches. The pastoral council and finance council are two instances of consultative organs at the parish level, but other means can also be provided to enable the Christian faithful to express their needs, desires, and opinions to their pastors (c. 212).

Consultation acknowledges that God's Spirit and wisdom are present in the community of the faithful, and that the leaders must search them out. For that reason, consultation, whether required by the canons or not, must be carried out with openness and complete honesty. Those consulted must be fully informed, brought together to listen to one another, allowed a free exchange of views and thorough discussion, and they must give their opinions candidly and sincerely. When a consensus emerges, the leaders, in normal circumstances, will follow it.

When they feel obliged to do otherwise, they should explain their reasons.

Monarchical style or the exercise of authority in isolation from the faithful community is out of place in the churches.[22] It is at odds with the Spirit-filled and profoundly participative nature of the church.

LAYPERSONS AND THE POWER OF GOVERNANCE

The question of "lay jurisdiction" is related to participative authority, but it is a distinct and more specific issue. Canonists have warmly debated the question in recent decades, both before the revised *Code* and after its promulgation.[23]

The term "power of jurisdiction" *(potestas iurisdictionis)*, which was the preponderant canonical usage for centuries, has now been replaced by "power of governance" *(potestas regiminis)*. "Jurisdiction" appeared only nine times in all of the Council documents, and only five times in the 1983 *Code;* the expression is not used at all in the 1990 *Code of Canons for the Eastern Churches.* "Power of governance" has a broader meaning and carries less of an overtone of dominance. The Latin word for governance, *regimen* comes from the verb *regere,* which does not mean to rule over or to dominate, but rather to guide or direct, as a rider does a horse or the helmsman guides a ship.

This brief overview of "lay jurisdiction" or of the participation of laypersons in the church's power of governance begins with (1) the actual exercise of authority by nonordained persons presently and historically. Next it briefly explores some of (2) the discussions, both before and after the Council, of the exercise of authority by laypersons. Then it presents some of (3) the central theological teachings of the Second Vatican Council which justify and support this form of lay participation.

1) The present discussion of the issue of the use of the power of governance by laypersons starts with the actual situation in the churches. There are thousands of parishes and other local Catholic congregations throughout the world led by nonpriests.

Deacons, religious, laywomen and laymen are "in charge" of them. These ministers, the vast majority of whom are nonordained, have been assigned to or chosen by these communities, and they direct and coordinate the ministry within them.

Other contemporary examples of lay ministers who exercise legitimate authority in the church are well known: judges and defenders in diocesan tribunals, financial administrators of dioceses and parishes, superintendents and principals of schools, directors of social services and health care facilities, superiors in lay religious institutes.[24] The canons of the *Code* explicitly provide for many of these offices.[25] To pretend that these key leaders of the church's ministry do not share in the power of governance is to perpetuate a fiction.

Many historical examples of the exercise of "jurisdiction" or the power of governance by those not ordained are well known:

- the leaders of the "house churches" in the first century were usually the householders who welcomed and hosted the congregations in their homes;
- the Christian emperors of Rome convoked all of the early ecumenical councils and several enacted laws for the internal discipline of the church;
- feudal landlords freely appointed priests as pastors of the churches located on their lands;
- medieval abbesses and prioresses not only supervised and directed the lives and properties of their monasteries and convents, but also granted faculties to confessors; some were accorded the dignity of archdeacons;
- popes granted jurisdiction to laypersons for various special tasks, for example, to act their legates or representatives or to serve as senior officials in the Roman Curia;
- from about the twelfth century ecclesiastical jurisdiction was generally limited to those in the clerical state, which was entered by the rite of tonsure (up until 1972), not by ordination; it was not unknown for tonsured but nonordained clerics to hold ecclesiastical offices.

2) There is precedent aplenty for lay exercise of the power of governance in the church. The present canonical restriction which limits the *possession* of this form of authority to the ordained, yet affirms the ambiguous *sharing in the exercise* of the power by laypersons[26] is purely and merely positive ecclesiastical law, not an intrinsic limitation or one based on "divine law."

It was common and official teaching (reiterated by Pope Pius XII as recently as 1957) that should a layperson be elected pope, upon acceptance he possessed the full authority of the office, even the charism of infallibility, before he was ordained. Similarly, a layman appointed or elected bishop received the full power of jurisdiction from the time of taking possession of the diocese, even if it was prior to his ordination.

After the Council, in December 1976, the Congregation for the Doctrine of the Faith responded to the question:

> Whether lay people, in as much as they have been made participants in their own way in the *munera* of Christ by baptism, can be assumed under the command of the bishops to some *munera* of governance or jurisdiction, namely those entailing participation in legislative, executive, or judicial powers.

The Congregation's answer, approved by Pope Paul VI, was:

> Dogmatically lay persons are excluded only from offices that are intrinsically hierarchical, the capacity for which is tied to the reception of the sacrament of orders.[27]

When the Commission for the Revision of the Code met in its final plenary session in October 1981, this issue of lay exercise of the power of governance was the first item on the agenda. An overwhelming majority of the Commission members voted in favor of the provisions, now in the 1983 *Code*, which permit the exercise.[28]

3) The documents of the Second Vatican Council provide ample theological warrant for the possession and use of the power of governance by laypersons. The wider range of theological themes includes: God's call; sacraments of initiation; full membership in God's people and Christ's body; sharing in

Christ's threefold priestly, prophetic, and kingly functions; active participation in and responsibility for the church's mission and ministry; and finally, the grace, power, and gifts of the Holy Spirit bestowed in abundance. A few of the more salient citations are presented here.

The Holy Spirit dwells in the entire church, sanctifies it, leads it to the truth, and unifies it in communion and ministry. The Spirit renews the church and leads it toward its ultimate union with Christ (*LG* 4). By baptism and participation in the Eucharist all are brought into communion with Christ and with one another, all are fully members of his body (*LG* 7).

> In the structure of the body of Christ, too, there is a diversity of members and of functions. There is one Spirit who distributes his various gifts for the good of the church according to his own riches and the needs of the ministries (see 1 Cor 12, 1–11). (*LG* 7)

Christ gives his followers a share in his Spirit, who is one and the same in head and members. This Spirit enlivens, unites, and moves the whole body of the church (LG 7).

> Moreover, the same Holy Spirit not only sanctifies and guides the people of God by means of the sacraments and the ministries and adorns it with virtues, he also apportions his gifts "to each individually as he wills" (1 Cor 12, 11), and among the faithful of every rank he distributes special graces by which he renders them fit and ready to undertake the various tasks and offices which help the renewal and the building up of the church, according to that word: "To each is given the manifestation of the Spirit for the common good" (1 Cor 12, 7). These charismatic gifts...are primarily suited to and useful for the needs of the church. (*LG* 12)

> [The laity] that is to say, the faithful who, since they have been incorporated into Christ by baptism, constitute the people of God and, in their own way participate in Christ's priestly, prophetic and royal function, exercise their own role in the mission of the whole Christian people in the church and in the world. (*LG* 31)

The laity are called to work for the growth of the church and its continual sanctification.

> The laity can also be called in various ways to a more immediate cooperation...like those men and women who assisted the apostle Paul in the gospel, working hard in the Lord (see Ph 4, 3; Rm 16, 3ff.). They may also be appointed by the hierarchy to carry out certain ecclesiastical offices *(munera)* which have a spiritual purpose. (*LG* 33)

> Jesus Christ...wants to continue his witness and service also through the laity, so he gives them life through his Spirit and unceasingly urges them on to every good and perfect work.
> He associates them intimately with his life and mission....The laity, therefore, dedicated as they are to Christ and anointed by the Holy Spirit, are wonderfully called and instructed so that ever more abundant fruits of the Spirit may be produced in them. (*LG* 34)

> The laity can and must perform the valuable task of evangelizing the world. Some lay people, when there is a shortage of sacred ministers or when they are impeded by a persecuting government, supply some of the sacred offices *(sacra officia)* in so far as they can; a greater number are engaged totally in apostolic work. (*LG* 35)

> The sacred pastors are to acknowledge and promote the dignity and the responsibility of the laity in the church; they should willingly make use of their prudent counsel; they should confidently entrust to them offices *(officia)* in the service of the church and leave them freedom and space to act. Indeed they should encourage them to take up work on their own initiative. (*LG* 37)

> The Holy Spirit...gives special gifts to the faithful....Thus, "as all use whatever gifts they have received in service to one another," they may be "good stewards dispensing the grace of God in its varied forms" (1 Pet 4, 10), towards the building up of the whole body in love (see Eph 4, 16). Through receiving these gifts of grace, however unspectacular, everyone of the faithful has the right and duty *(ius et officium)* to

exercise them in the church and in the world for the good of humanity and for the building up of the church. (*AA* 3; see also *AA* 1 and 2)

All of the aforementioned current practices, historical examples, and conciliar themes, taken individually or together, are more than adequate to sustain the possession and exercise of authority in the church on the part of laypersons. In fact, it is hard to envision any limit on lay exercise of the power of governance, short of that immediately attached to the episcopal office.

The actual selection, preparation, and recognition of laypersons for these tasks is another matter. Persons have vastly different gifts and talents, different levels of intelligence, ability, and training. The gifts of the Spirit must be carefully discerned, and ample formation for ministries provided. Not everyone who walks down Main Street should minister at St. Mary's, but neither should they be considered unqualified for ministry or responsibility because they are not ordained.

In Conclusion

The common good of every human community requires good order. Paul urged those in Corinth not to be childish in their outlook, but mature. Everything must be done with a constructive purpose, for building up, and not only so that outsiders will not consider the followers of Christ Jesus to be out of their minds (1 Cor 14, 20ff.).

In the church there are even more profound reasons for doing things "in good order."[29] The church is a human community which is at the same time a sacrament of salvation. It shows forth the mystery of God's love for humanity (*LG* 9). The communal structure of the church serves Christ's Spirit (*LG* 8). This means that local congregations as well as the church's administrative structures, for example, dioceses, episcopal conferences, the papal Curia, all must act, speak, and be seen as components of the sacrament of God's love. Authority exercised within these structures exists essentially for the building up of the community, for service to local congregations, and as witness to the world.

Canonical ministry constantly engages and exerts authority. Whether it is in the appointment of pastors, the settlement of disputes, the formulation of liturgical or ecumenical policies, or the granting of dispensations, nearly all canonical activities are related to the exercise of authority in the churches. That authority must be in service to the church. It must be exercised only in ways that are in keeping with the reality of the church: a sacrament of salvation and sign of God's love for humanity.

CHAPTER 7

CANON LAW AS MINISTRY

CANON LAW IS, BEFORE ALL ELSE, a ministry within the church. Canon Law is also an area of study, an organized body of knowledge, an academic discipline, a sacred science. But more than any of these, it specifies and names one of the church's salient ministries, the ministry of freedom and good order.

Canon Law is something that people *do* in and for the church. After men and women study it and learn it, they *practice* it, they *perform* its functions and duties for the benefit of believers and their communities. Canon Law is an ancient and highly valued ministry in the Catholic Church.

This chapter examines the ministry of Canon Law from various aspects: 1) what it is that canonists do today, 2) the New Testament notion of the gift of good guidance, 3) what ministry is, 4) how ministry has evolved, 5) how Canon Law relates to other disciplines, 6) how it relates to other ministries, 7) Canon Law as a science, 8) canonical education, and 9) a gospel admonition about the hazards of the ministry.

WHAT CANONISTS DO

One way to envision Canon Law as ministry is to look at what canonists do, what activities they engage in. "Canonists" are those who have earned academic degrees in Canon Law and are actively engaged in its exercise. What is it that they actually do?

Most of them serve in diocesan tribunals.[1] About half of all professional canonists (at least in North America) work, full- or part-time, in matrimonial tribunals in the roles of judicial vicars, judges, or defenders of the bond. Many others, around 20 percent, function in the church's administrative offices, for example, as vicars general, chancellors, moderators of the Curia, secretaries to bishops. Another 20 percent are pastors, chaplains, rectors, or administrators of parishes. Many canonists serve as bishops or religious superiors, or they act as counselors to bishops or provincial superiors. A relatively few canonists, about 5 percent, teach Canon Law to those preparing for various ministries in the church, for example, in seminaries or theological centers, or to those preparing for the canonical ministry itself. All of these men and women are actively engaged in the practice of Canon Law. They work at one or more of the various specialties within the ministry of Canon Law.

One other feature of canonical practice deserves special mention. Canonists are most often sponsored for study and then employed by dioceses or religious communities.[2] These connections and the loyalties they engender can cause canonists to shift the focus of their ministry from local church communities and the individual believers within them to the institutions which actually support the canonists. In this situation canonists may become less concerned about freedom and good order within the church as the objects of their ministry, and instead become focused on the protection and promotion of their own diocese, religious community, or educational institution.[3]

This institutional loyalty is understandable, but canonists must always bear in mind the common good of the church (c. 223). In their ministry canonists must first attend to the nature and mission of the church, and to the primary expressions of church, local congregations of the faithful. The canonical ministry is at the service of the churches and their members. Public ministry is never merely "private practice" nor solely attentive to the interests of the sponsor-employer.

THE GIFT OF GOOD GUIDANCE

Another way to envision Canon Law as ministry is to start with the "spiritual gifts" given to the churches by the Holy Spirit, those gifts enumerated by the Apostle Paul. Paul's most complete inventory of these God-given forms of service to the church appears in chapter 12 of his first letter to the Corinthians. Well down on the list[4] is the gift of guidance or leadership. Paul's Greek word is *kubernesis,* which literally means "those who direct or lead," from the verb *kubernein,* to steer or pilot a ship. It is the same word used in the Book of Proverbs for "sound guidance," as in "an intelligent person will gain sound guidance" (1, 5) or "for lack of guidance a people falls" (11, 14).

In his letter to the church at Corinth, Paul spoke of that gift or combination of qualities which enable a Christian to give wise and sound direction to a congregation, to guide or govern it in an orderly way. The gift of good guidance, like all of the other "manifestations of the Spirit," is given for the common good (v. 7). It would be absurdly anachronistic to suggest that Paul was referring to canonists when he spoke of this role of leadership. Most likely he had in mind persons like Aquila, Prisca (1 Cor 16, 19), or Philemon, who were householders and probably leaders of the churches which met in their homes.

In the long Catholic tradition since Paul's time, however, a refined sense of church order and the "canons" which express that order has held a high place among the valued talents or skills for church leaders. For example, the canons have long specified Canon Law as one of the academic areas of qualification for episcopal candidates.[5] There are other, more precious gifts, like those of prophecy (proclaiming God's word) and of teaching (explaining the word) necessary for leadership of the community, but a sense of wise and orderly direction has always been prized.

Paul's metaphor of the helmsman[6] implies much more than a person steering a ship. The one who "takes the helm" must know not only the ship and the ocean, the weather, stars, and shoals, but the captain, crew, and cargo. To guide the ship aright also requires a knowledge of the rules of the high seas, for example, which ship has the right of way. The canonist, who knows the church and its rules and how to apply them in guiding the community, is a helmsman.

Finally, Paul did not envision leadership (good guidance) or any of the other gifts or ministries on his list as either isolated or in opposition to one another. Rather all of them come from the same source (Spirit, Lord, God), and all are to work together in mutual interdependence. They are to function as parts of the same body, that is, the body of Christ, and are given for the common good which benefits the community.[7]

"Everything should be done for building up...everything must be done properly and in good order."[8] The canonist's ministry of freedom and order exists to foster that vital collaboration for the good of the churches, for the sake of St. Mary's on Main Street.

WHAT IS A MINISTRY?

"Ministry" is the generic term used to describe the functions or services performed within the church. It applies to those works and services irrespective of whether they are performed by laypersons, members of religious institutes, or the ordained. The meaning of "ministry" comes from the Greek word *diakonia,* which is used in the New Testament in the same generic sense of "forms of service" (e.g., in 1 Cor 12, 5) as well as with more specialized meanings. *Ministerium,* meaning service, assistance, or office, is the Latin equivalent.

Ministry describes public activity, performed by baptized members of the church, under the impetus of the Spirit's gifts, recognized or affirmed by the community, in service to the kingdom of God. Ministries assist in the upbuilding of the community of faith, hope, and love. They aid in the community's witness to and struggle toward the realization of God's design for the world. Ministry is usually associated with the proclamation of the word, the celebration of sacraments, or works of charity. Ministry enables the community in its fulfillment of Christ's threefold mission of teaching, sanctifying, and ruling.

Ministries are now and always have been specified in a multitude of modes. Some are full-time and full-salaried, requiring years of professional preparation, while others are part-time and voluntary, and call for relatively little formal training. They range from the highly visible and powerful offices of bishop and pastor to the modest roles of greeter, usher, choir member, and altar server. All these ministries involve human activity, prompted by the Holy Spirit, performed in Christ's name, on behalf of a Christian community, and are for the sake of God's kingdom.

Ministries are not few and fixed. They are numerous and variable. There have always been dozens of different ministries in the church. The New Testament tells of more than a score: apostles, prophets, teachers, wisdom-speakers, knowledge-speakers, miracle workers, healers, helpers, administrators, speakers in tongues, interpreters of tongues, distinguishers of spirits, admonishers, benefactors, deacons, evangelists, pastors, elders, overseers, and others.

Some of those early ministerial roles were inadequately distinct. For example, the functions of elders (presbyters, *presbyteroi*) and overseers (supervisors, *episkopoi*) are used interchangeably in the Pastoral Letters. The ministries were not precisely defined or clearly differentiated. Some ministries were in place in some local churches and were unknown in others. Many were formed in response to community needs, and their names and structures depended on local cultural contexts. The selection of "the seven" to assist with the daily distribution of food to the widows in the church at Jerusalem (Acts 6, 1–6) is perfect example. The New Testament period was obviously a formative time of development and change for the churches and their ministries.

CHANGE AND CONTROL

The church's ministries continued to change and develop well beyond New Testament times. In fact, ministerial roles continued to develop, to atrophy, to disappear, and sometimes even to reappear throughout history. Ministry has always been and remains a changing scene, just at it is at St. Mary's on Main Street today. There have been periods of relative stability, but change has been more constant than stasis. A few examples will underscore the relatively fluid nature of the church's ministries:

1) As the churches survived and multiplied during the first decades after the death and resurrection of Jesus, their "authority structures" or "leadership arrangements" shifted several times:

- from church communities living in and led by the Spirit (Gal 5, 25) and ordered by the Spirit's multifold gifts (Rom 12, 6–8),
- to Paul's prioritized sequence of "apostles, prophets, and teachers" (1 Cor 12, 28), of Jewish derivation,
- to a later listing of "evangelists, pastors, and teachers" (Eph 4, 11), probably a transitional pattern, and then
- to the roles of "ministers *(diakonai),* overseers *(episkopoi),* and elders *(presbyteroi)*" in the Pastoral Letters, which bore Greek titles, but did not yet convey the meanings or relationships they would later inherit.

It was not until the middle or late second century that the enduring and familiar pattern of bishop-presbyter-deacon emerged. Its most common operational form consisted of a college of presbyters which exercised supervision in the local church. One of their number, thenceforth called *episkopos* (bishop), was chosen to preside. The deacons were usually in charge of administration of property and distribution of charity (the original role of "the seven" in Acts 6). The "monarchical episcopate," wherein the bishop exercised authority with relative autonomy, was a later development.

2) Deacons *(diakonoi)* exercised a variety of functions throughout history. In some early periods a deacon or archdeacon served as the bishop's "right-hand man," his messenger, information-gatherer, and the organizer of ministry to the poor.

But gradually the deacon's role was restricted to liturgical service, and then it became a mere stepping-stone on the way to the presbyterate. The Second Vatican Council restored the diaconate, but left it to individual bishops' conferences or Eastern churches to decide whether it was opportune to reinstate the order within their territories (*LG* 29, *OE* 17). The subsequent development of the "permanent diaconate" in various nations and even in various dioceses within them has differed dramatically; there are thousands of deacons in some parts of the world whereas they are virtually unknown in others.

3) In 1972 Pope Paul VI completely suppressed the order of the subdiaconate as well as the minor orders of exorcist and acolyte.[9] All of these orders had been at one time actively functioning ministries within the local churches, but long ago they had become merely symbolic steps on the road toward presbyteral ordination.

4) The episcopate, despite its long and distinguished history, was for many centuries not considered to be one of the "holy orders" in the ordinary teaching of the church. The seven orders were porter, lector, acolyte, exorcist, subdeacon, deacon, and presbyter. The episcopate was an added dignity, a part of the church's hierarchy, but not a sacramental order, since it added nothing to the priesthood in its relationship to the Eucharist, that is, in celebrating Mass a bishop "does no more than a priest." The Second Vatican Council rehabilitated the episcopate, redescribed it as the fullness of the sacrament of orders, and placed it at the apex of sacred ministry (*LG* 21).

5) Many of the ministries named in the New Testament, for example, speakers in tongues, interpreters of tongues, admonishers, miracle workers, and healers, are no longer recognized as public ministries in the church, even though some of their functions are sustained in some communities.

The growth and decline of the church's ministries, their variety and reinterpretations, are not signs of weakness, disorder, or instability. Rather the phenomenon highlights the suppleness and adaptability of ministry. It demonstrates the church's vitality and ability to respond to pastoral needs and altered social situations.

Above all, the changing names and identities of ministry reveal that they are firmly under the church's control. Local and particular churches form and shape their ministries to suit their needs. This is true of ministries that are considered to be sacramental as well as those which are not within the sacrament of orders.

Jesus Christ, who was the originating inspiration of the church, did not design or establish a set of ministerial roles or offices. There is no evidence of such a permanent blueprint from the Lord. Hence the church's ministries are never fixed, crystallized, set in stone. Quite the contrary, they are malleable, pliable, flexible. Christ sent the Holy Spirit to guide and care for his people, and, under the Spirit's deft direction the churches fashion and refashion their ministries.

CANON LAW RELATED TO OTHER DISCIPLINES

Canon Law as a ministry and as an academic discipline does not stand in isolation, but relates to and depends upon other ministries and disciplines. It is quite clearly a theological discipline, and as such, it draws from and interacts with other areas of theological studies: a) sacred scripture, b) church history, c) systematic and historical theology, especially d) ecclesiology, and e) moral theology.

Sacred Scripture

The scriptures contain God's revelation, most centrally God's own loving Self-revelation. They are the primary source for the knowledge and understanding of God's new and definitive covenant with humankind in Christ (*DV* 4). The written word of God is the church's first rule of faith and rule of life. Hence it goes without saying that Canon Law, like the church itself, stands under and depends upon sacred scripture. Even the supreme teaching authority is not above the word of God, but serves it, teaching only that which is handed down (*DV* 10).

The canonist needs not only a broad knowledge of the scriptures, but a carefully honed scientific understanding of and deep familiarity with them. There is no room in Canon Law for simplistic "proof-texts" or superficial applications of the scriptures, just as there is no place for biblical fundamentalism. Canon Law must be based on an understanding of scripture which is contemporary and perennial, sophisticated, and prayerful.

> "What was handed down from the apostles" includes everything that helps the people of God to lead a holy life and to grow in faith. In this way, the church, in its teaching, life and worship, perpetuates and hands on to every generation all that it is and all that it believes. (*DV* 8)

The positive provisions of the canons must always be viewed against the rich background of this tradition which comes from the apostles and progresses under the assistance of the Holy Spirit. Its study and contemplation leads to a growth in understanding of what is handed on, both the words and the reality they signify (*DV* 8).

> The word of God, which is the power of God for salvation to everyone who has faith, is presented and shows its force preeminently in the writings of the New Testament. (*DV* 17)

> There is such force and power in the word of God that it stands as the church's support and strength, affording her children sturdiness in faith, food for the soul, and a pure and unfailing fount of the spiritual life. (*DV* 21)

Canon Law should call upon this power of the word of God. The canons themselves should embody scriptural texts and thus afford a source of biblical nourishment and strength. Canonical themes and practices, and even the very language of the *Codes,* should be linked to and expressed in the words of their biblical sources, when that is possible. Canonical language is more frequently drawn from Roman law and secular juridic practice than it is from the scriptures. A return to a more biblical expression for the canons would give them greater authenticity, and allow the people of the church to hear in the canons the resonance of God's holy word, rather than language borrowed from civil law courts.[10]

The canons are, like any set of regulations, also a source of learning. They educate the members of the community about the values of the community. In the church the rules should, to the extent possible and reasonable, be a part of that ongoing repast, the sharing of the bread of life at the table of the word of God. The rules should be expressed in the recognized language of the Christian tradition, the supreme rule of faith (*DV* 21). They should employ the cherished language, the words, phrases, and images of the Bible itself.

Church History

As the local communities of believers called churches lived and prayed and witnessed through the centuries, they adopted practices and customs, they obeyed and disregarded rules, they organized their congregations and their sacramental lives. Canon Law represents those "organizational" aspects of their story. Echoes of this canonical voice are heard within the story, to the extent that it is remembered and retold in the history of the church.

History chronicles and interprets the life of the churches and their place in the world around them. It reminds us of the rulers who persecuted the early churches, those who exploited the churches to benefit their own secular kingdoms, and those who aided and enhanced the churches for the sake of God's kingdom. History tells of destructive divisions, of bitter debates, of heroic exploits, of amazing missionary efforts, in short, of the life and times of believing people gathered into churches.

Canon Law was a part of it all. Canonists fought on both sides of all the battles, and worked on all the peace treaties. Church history records their participation, the rules made and broken, the wise regulations and the foolish ones, the clever negotiations and the fruitless ones. It is by attending to the historical record that today's canonist tries to avoid making the same mistakes. Canon Law relies constantly on the history of the churches which it serves.

Theology

Canon Law is to theology as horticulture is to botany, as the practice of medicine is to the science of physiology. It is the theology of the church put into practice. Canon Law is a subset of theology, not a subset of law or juridical science. Canon Law is applied theology. It expresses in norms and rules and practices what the church believes and teaches about itself. Canon Law gives institutional expression to the faith of the Christian community.

Canon Law is derived from theology. When the church deepens and changes its understanding of its own belief, then the rules must be changed or at least applied differently. For example, when the church's understanding of the sacrament of confirmation changes, then the regulation governing the age at which sacrament is to be received must change as well. When the church experiences the effective ministry of women, the rules prohibiting them from ordination are called into question.

Theology as a science is an organized body of knowledge about God. Thomas Aquinas called theology a reasoned mode of understanding according to revelation.[11] Christian systematic theology, as a project or exercise, is the ongoing attempt to explain beliefs using some philosophical method or organizing principle, for example, Platonism, Aristotelianism, existentialism, linguistic analysis, or a theory of liberation. Theology focuses on God's revelation, both as perceived through the inspired scriptures and received in the subsequent tradition, and tries to make sense of it for contemporary believers. Historical theology focuses on the authors or schools of a given period in the past by using historical methods of analysis.

A plurality of theologies complicates the task of Canon Law. Throughout the history of the church there have been many theological visions, not just one or a few. Augustine differed with Jerome on some matters, and Thomas and Bonaventure took different approaches. Whole schools and traditions have existed and still exist alongside one another in a very large and widespread church, for example, the mystical and monastic traditions, the Eastern Christian traditions, liturgical and patristic theologies. The question arises, Which one does Canon Law use as a norm at any given time?

Canon Law, at least in its general or "universal" norms, must operate on the basis of some theological consensus. Otherwise it tumbles into the pit of pure positivism, that is, the rule is whatever the rule-maker says it is at any given time. When there is little theological consensus, as in times of ferment, then canonists must foster freedom for the sake of the common good. The "reason for the law" (the *ratio legis*) must make sense to the people if the rule is going to be received and observed. There must be a credible theological position on which to ground the rule.

When coherent explanations for a rule of action are not forthcoming, then the community must limp along on the crutch of formal authority, a weak prop indeed! When the church teaches one thing and its rules say another, confusion abounds. For example, the Vatican Council described the sacrament of marriage as a covenant, but the canons still treat it as a consensual contract after the old pattern of Roman law. It is a case not only of cognitive dissonance (conflicting theories), but operational dissonance as well. The validity of marriage contracts are adjudicated by standards which differ in part from the Council's teaching about marriage, for example, in respect to the good of the spouses, the import of married love, a partnership of the whole of life (*GS* 48–50).

Another example is the Council's teaching that the College of Bishops has supreme and full power over the universal church (*LG* 22), but the canons leave the college without any effective way of exercising that authority between ecumenical councils.

One more illustration: God's universal salvific will is bedrock church teaching, a fundamental theological presupposition. "God…wills everyone to be saved and to come to knowledge of the truth" (1 Tm 2, 4). If the canons set up barriers to church membership based on caste, personal status (e.g., free or slave), literacy, or the ability to make an offering, it would amount to a contradiction of that basic doctrine.

Canon Law is dependent upon theology, but the dependence is not abject. Canon Law also made and makes important contributions to theology. It was by borrowing canonical methods for the interpretation of texts that Peter Abelard laid the foundations for the scholastic renewal of theology in the early twelfth century. Canons and other disciplinary norms have constituted a *locus theologicus* from the beginning. That is to say, the churches' practices and rules of discipline have served as evidence of the churches' faith from the earliest times, for example, the date of Easter, the nonrepeatability of baptism, and orders.

Ecclesiology

The structure, provisions, and interpretation of Canon Law are most directly related to the area of theology known as ecclesiology. The church's order and discipline must accurately reflect theological convictions about the church's nature and mission in the world. It is a fact almost too obvious to assert.

The Second Vatican Council, when treating the formation of candidates for the presbyterate, clearly affirmed this connection between Canon Law and ecclesiolgy:

> In the exposition of canon law...attention must be paid to the mystery of the church, according to the dogmatic constitution "On the church" promulgated by this holy synod. (*OT* 16)

Like all other theological disciplines Canon Law also is to be "taught in the light of faith" and "renewed by a more lively contact with the mystery of Christ and salvation history." It is to be learned in a context of ecumenical awareness and with sensitivity to other religions (*OT* 16).

Ecclesiology is an area of theology which developed relatively late, well after the reflections on God, the Trinity, Christ, grace, and even the sacraments. The first treatises on the theology of the church were written in the fourteenth century. The canonical tradition is much older than that. Canon Law was a well-developed profession and area of scientific study by the fourteenth century. However, now at the beginning of the third millennium, it is transparently evident that Canon Law must be governed by ecclesiology.

Problems arise when the theology of the church is not consistent or not entirely coherent within itself. For example, *Lumen Gentium* and other documents of the Council which describe the church are the products of compromises, and they contain unresolved conflicts and deliberate ambiguities. Within this context it is a commonplace to recognize "two ecclesiolgies" in the Council documents: one of the church as sacrament and communion, the other of the church as a juridically "perfect society" comparable to the Republic of Venice.

This "conflict of ecclesiologies" is a principal cause of the inadequacy of the 1983 *Code of Canon Law*. Theological development since the Vatican Council has largely resolved the conflict in favor of the "church as sacrament and communion." Now it is time to renew the *Code* in conformity with that theology. To continue to use a theologically compromised *Code* is to risk further distortions of the church's nature and functions. For example, an assertion of the rights and duties of local churches (e.g., parishes) within the particular churches (dioceses) is almost entirely absent from the *Code*, yet the local communities of the faithful are the primary reality of the church.

Moral Theology

Canon Law and moral theology were once wed, but the marriage was not a happy one. Moral theology did not develop as a separate area of Christian theology dealing with human conscience and actions until the sixteenth century. Since it focused on providing confessors with specific answers to questions of conscience, moral theology tended to look to law for guidance. A large part of the content of moral theology consisted of canonical obligations: the commandments of the church, the regulation of the sacraments, the church's laws on crimes and punishments. These topics were taught as major parts of moral theology, to such an extent that they were often left out of seminary courses on Canon Law.

Moreover, moral methodology was greatly influenced by legalistic attitudes, with a focus on minimal obedience to external authority rather than the cultivation of a truly Christian spirit. While moral theology became legalized, Canon Law became privatized, and concerned with individual conscience rather than the common good. Many of its rules were overvalued and given exaggerated importance; ordinary regulations became "divine law by association" by a sort of canonical halo effect. For example, it was considered to be a mortal sin to omit one hour of the Divine Office without sufficient cause.

Moral theology and Canon Law parted ways after the Vatican Council, and both have developed in healthier directions since then. Moral theology now draws on the authentic sources of scripture and tradition and the signs of the times to identify and teach values appropriate for contemporary Christian living, while Canon Law has recentered its attention on general norms for the church's communal life in the external forum. Both offer guidance to the members of the church; however, they do this in quite different ways. But moral theology and Canon Law must remain on good speaking terms. The values they both seek for the church are aligned, for example, together the two disciplines foster loving care within the community. Their cordial cooperation is vital for the life of the churches.

CANON LAW AND OTHER MINISTRIES

Canon Law can be compared to other ministries of the church, many of which are also ancient and necessary. Like these other ministries, Canon Law is theological in its orientation, that is, it is based on God's revelation and the community's reflective understanding of that revelation, but it borrows some of its methods from sources outside theology. The following are some examples of comparable ministries together with a suggestion of their related methodological tools: a) preaching, b) catechesis, c) liturgical celebration, d) pastoral counseling, and e) administration.

Preaching

No ministry in the church is more central, more vitally important, or more universally necessary than the proclamation of God's word which is called preaching. It is key to every form of Christian worship, and a primary means of formation and reinforcement in faith. Obviously, preaching presupposes knowledge of the scriptures and of the church's theological tradition, as well as an awareness of the local community. But effective preaching also draws upon logic, rhetoric, and elocution. The arts of public speaking, orderly discourse, and persuasive argumentation are all required for this ministry. These "secular" sciences and skills are the means by which the preacher carries out his or her ministry.

Catechesis

Similarly, the faith formation which Christians experience from their earliest years and all through adulthood, in the continuous resounding echo of God's word, in oral and written instruction, and the handing on of all that has been received in and through Christ, is a ministry of primary importance within every Christian community. Those who engage in the critical catechetical function must also be imbued with the scriptures and the breadth of the theological tradition. However, they must know and employ a modern understanding of educational philosophy, developmental psychology, and instructional and motivational skills as well. In other words, teaching methods and learning theories common to all forms of education and formation are essential to the ministry of catechesis.

Liturgical Celebration

Worship, of course, is at the heart of the Christian community's life, the source of its activity. In this sense, it is the work, the action of the entire community, and of every member. Full and active participation in the liturgy is the first sign of communion, of meaningful membership in the church. However, as a ministry, as a "specialty" within the church's panoply of official functions, it requires both ability and training. Planning, coordinating, and leading liturgical celebrations calls for a deep knowledge of Christian tradition, especially its biblical, theological, spiritual, and sacramental dimensions. Just as knowledge of the canons is critical in canonical ministry, so a close familiarity with the church's official liturgical books is essential for liturgical ministry. But real liturgical ministry also requires a sense of symbol, movement, posture, and gesture, of the dynamics of assemblies, music, space, and light. It draws upon these and other areas of human knowledge, skill, and artistry.

Pastoral Counseling

The frequent and varied personal encounters with individuals and families within local churches call forth a range of pastoral abilities. Whether it is a "crisis intervention" or a simple request for advice, the consolation of the bereaved or help with an ordinary family problem, these pastoral opportunities require a keen sense of the Christian tradition, especially its ethical and moral dimensions. But counseling also demands listening and attending skills; an understanding of human development, family dynamics, and elements of psychology, normal and abnormal; and a knowledge of additional local resources. In sum, this pastoral ministry of the church necessarily employs certain "secular" areas of knowledge and skills for its proper performance.

Administration

The responsible care for church personnel and property has been and is another necessary ministry. Funds, property, employees, volunteers, and all of the other material necessities of church life must be looked after, organized, utilized well, and accounted for. The ministry of church administration demands a well-developed sense of the church itself, its nature, mission, and local operation. However, good administration also requires a knowledge of accounts, budgets, property maintenance, employment policies and practices, insurance, and legal liabilities. In other words, church administration calls for management skills in addition to a sense of responsibility and social justice.

In Conclusion

Each of these ministries is specified by its context: it operates within the saving community of the faithful which is called church. The purpose and function of each is qualified and conditioned because it is a ministry within the church.

Everyone who ministers in the Roman Catholic Church must know and be able to perform each of these basic ministries with some measure of ability and skill. All of these ministries are needed at St. Mary's on Main Street. In each diocese, however, there should be some persons, lay or ordained, who are truly learned and expert in these key areas of ministry. These specially trained ministers guide and support the others.

In this sense, canonical ministry is like the other ministries. Everyone who ministers in the church needs to know some Canon Law, and a few persons need to know it very well. These few need to have advanced training and comprehensive knowledge about the canonical tradition, about the rules and structures according to which the church operates, and about the necessary zones of freedom, personal responsibility, and pastoral discretion.

As a ministry within the church, Canon Law is a means to an end, namely the free and orderly life of the churches and their members. It is an instrument in service to the saving purpose of the church. It is an aid toward the attainment of the mission of the church: teaching, sanctifying and guiding in the name of Christ and under the impulse of the Holy Spirit.

CANON LAW AS A SCIENCE

Canon Law is a "sacred science" like biblical studies, systematic and moral theology, and church history. It is an organized body of knowledge with a long and distinguished tradition, in addition to its primary identity as a ministry. The subject matter of Canon Law is concerned with members of the church, their rights and duties, ministries within the church, those qualified to exercise them, sacraments, church buildings and property, teaching authority, church governance, settlement of disputes, and the meting out of punishment, all within the context of the church.

Sacred Science and Divine Law

The various theological fields of study are referred to as "sacred sciences" because they deal with sacred things, that is, with God, God's actions in the world, and the church and its ministries. Canon Law is a sacred science in that sense, but its individual rules or canons are human, not divine. The canons are "sacred" only in the sense that they treat of persons and matters which are considered to be sacred. The canons are not part of God's revelation. They are human regulations which are more or less related to or based on that revelation. They are not sacred because they come from God or because they bring salvation. The canons are not bearers of grace, nor do they accomplish sanctification. They are quite simply the rules which govern the life and activity of the churches and their ministries.

Nearly all of the canons are mutable; they have changed and will change again. One way that canonists distinguish the rules which will not or cannot change from those which can and will, is by calling the former "divine law" *(ius divinum).* "Divine laws" were thought to be so directly and immediately based on divine revelation or on the "natural law," that is, on the very structure which the Creator gave to things, that they were like laws given by God. The label "divine law" meant that the rule was irreversible, permanent, and immutable. The name lent a vastly exaggerated importance to a canon, as though it came from the very hand of God. But this category of "divine law" has expanded and contracted over the centuries, and it continues to shift and change.[12] As a category it is so ambiguous and misleading as to be no longer serviceable. The canonical category of "divine law" should be abandoned.

Indeed, the documents of the Second Vatican Council did not once use the expression "divine law." The 1983 *Code* uses the expression only eight times.[13] In most instances the term is so vague as to be virtually meaningless. Even when referring to matrimonial impediments, there is no enduring consensus on which are "divine law" and which are "merely ecclesiastical law" (c. 11).[14]

The *Code* employs the term *lex divina* only six times,[15] and the meanings are similarly vague and indeterminate. In all instances the canonical usage of "divine law" gives the false impression that some of the church's rules actually come directly from God.

A Theological Discipline

As a science or discipline or field of study, Canon Law is a subset of theology. It is not a species of the genus law.[16] Canon Law receives its principles, guidance, and illumination from the scriptures and from the church's tradition. It depends on theological teachings: on Christology, on pneumatology, Christian anthropology, sacramental theology, and most immediately and directly on ecclesiology, the theology of the church itself.

Canon Law is at the service of the communion of the churches. It provides for their normative organization, it supplies their ordering structures, it is the instrument of their just social order.[17]

The *Codes* of Canon Law, the primary sources for the church's rules today, are regarded as handbooks for the guidance of the church's ministers, its bishops and pastors. The *Codes* do serve that function, but the canons they contain are not principally for the sake of ministers, they are there for the well-being of the *churches*. The canons provide guidance for decisions about policies, procedures, and practical actions, in short, direction for the lives and activities of local churches and the people who belong to them. Canon Law exists mainly to serve local congregations and their members.

Canon Law is a means to the end of the church, whether that end is expressed in terms of the *salus animarum*, the salvation of souls, or the *sacramentum mundi*, the sign of God's love for the world.[18] Canon Law must never be viewed as an end in itself.

Finally, Canon Law contains the church's fundamental structures as well as its more changeable positive rules. That is to say, it expresses both a "constitutional order" for the church and particular regulations for its life and activities. Canon Law describes a core juridical structure which grounds its more transitory statutory provisions.[19] Obviously, the fundamental structure is more closely tied to the theology of the church than are the particular, transient rules. For example, the linking of local churches together by the multiple bonds of communion defines the very structure of the church, but the way that the pastors of those churches are selected is variable and has changed greatly over time.

A Juridical Science?

Canon Law does present a juridical aspect, without doubt. It is like one of the visual prospects within a large park. Canon Law does stand for justice and fairness within the community of Christ. But that does not make Canon Law a juridical science. The purposes of canonical rules are much broader than to achieve justice: to maintain communion, promote participation, regulate sacraments, proclaim the word, discern charisms, encourage reconciliation, facilitate growth of faith, hope, and love.[20]

"Ubi societas ibi ius" is a true saying. Where human persons relate within any community, they and the community have rights. Those rights must be respected and defended, even vindicated on occasion. The church of Christ cannot be a zone of arbitrariness, of repression, or of irresponsible actions. The canons express the rights of members and communities and provide means for their protection. So, in this sense, Canon Law operates with a juridical methodology. Canon Law strives to see that everyone receives her or his due, *unicuique suum.* But it is not a juridical science, it is not a species or subset of law. It is a ministry within the church, one function of which is to see that justice is done.

"Juridicity," *ius publicum ecclesiasticum,* and the vision of the church as a perfect society are simply the wrong places to begin to describe Canon Law.[21] These concepts are derived from the secular legal and political order rather than from the church's own heritage of scripture and tradition. The canonical system is a set of internal rules for the governance of the church, and the church is *toto caelo* different from the state, which is the primary analogue for these concepts.

Similarly, to describe Canon Law as a theological discipline which employs a juridical methodology is misleading.[22] Canonists do often use juridical methods: laws are to be understood in keeping with the proper meaning of their words considered in their text and context, judges must make their decisions based on the evidence presented, acts performed under extreme duress have no effect.[23] But canonists also make use of exegetical, theological, historical, and pastoral methodologies as well. That is to say, in the process of making, interpreting, and applying regulations for the churches, canonical practitioners must call upon the methods of the other sacred sciences which rule Canon Law. Otherwise, the canonical science falls prey to narrow positivism or pure legalism.

To put it another way, canonists are not lawyers. Canonists are ministers of the church, and they make use of the resources, methods, and skills common to church ministry.

EDUCATION FOR CANONICAL MINISTRY

Most people initially encounter Canon Law in a program of theological studies for ministry in a seminary or university. This setting is entirely appropriate for an introduction to Canon Law, especially if the discipline has been "renewed by a livelier contact with the mystery of Christ and the history of salvation," as the Vatican Council's decree on priestly formation directed.[24] In the explanation of Canon Law "the mystery of the church should be kept in mind as it was set forth in the Dogmatic Constitution on the Church."[25] In other words, the essential context for the study of the church's canonical discipline is theological, and specifically Christological, soteriological, and ecclesiological.

Unfortunately, when it comes to the advanced study of Canon Law, the actual emphasis is quite different. These are the academic programs of study which lead to degrees that have canonical value, that is, they qualify their recipients for ecclesiastical offices such as those of judge or bishop.[26] These programs of graduate-level studies in Canon Law are offered exclusively in faculties canonically erected or approved by the Holy See. Their programs are closely regulated by norms issued by the pope and the Congregation for Catholic Education.[27] These courses of studies are overwhelmingly juridical in content rather than theological.

The programs of canonical studies emphasize the cultivation, promotion, and instruction in "the juridical disciplines" and "juridical formation."[28] The core of these programs is the "second cycle," that is, the two years of studies leading to the licentiate degree in Canon Law. The focus of this "second cycle" is entirely on the Code and other canonical laws, philosophy of law, public ecclesiastical law, Roman law, civil law, and the history of Canon Law.[29] In other words, the central focus of canonical studies is dominantly juridical and minimally biblical or theological. It is described in terms more suitable for legal studies than for ministerial preparation.

Elements of sacred theology ("especially of ecclesiology and sacramental theology") are required in the "first cycle" of canonical studies, but these are prerequisites, preliminary to actual engagement with the canons. Anyone who has completed the ordinary theological curriculum "in a seminary or in some other approved institution of higher learning" may proceed directly into the "second cycle" regardless of the quality of the theological program or when the person completed it.[30] Thus the prerequisite theological training can be remote, weak, or perfunctory.

It is only fair to note that the entire canonical program is supposed to be carried out "in the light of the law of the Gospel" so as to form those "trained to hold special ecclesiastical posts."[31]

However, the regulations also provide for a "fast track" for civil lawyers:

> A person who has already earned a doctorate in civil law, may be allowed...to abbreviate the course, always maintaining however the obligation to pass all the examinations and tests required for receiving academic degrees.[32]

This special provision in favor of civil lawyers, a peculiar feature in a program for church ministry, further emphasizes the essentially juridical nature of these programs of study.

The design of these programs of canonical education springs from another time and another perception of Canon Law, when it was conceived of as a juridical science within a church envisioned as a "perfect society." Even though the charter document for ecclesiastical faculties and their programs was revised since the Second Vatican Council, the content and design of its canonical degree programs are based on an earlier and outmoded vision of what canonists are and do. Indeed, it is remarkable to note that the 1979 *Sapientia Christiana* outline of the three "cycles" of canonical studies is almost exactly the same as the 1931 *Deus Scientiarum Dominus* version.[33] The content of the course of studies is virtually unchanged except for the substitution of one *Code of Canon Law* (1983) for another (1917).

Pope Paul VI made famous the need for a new way of thinking *(novus habitus mentis)*[34] for canonists after the Council. The pope urged in his addresses that the old ways of juridicism and formalism had to be abandoned, and that canonical studies must rise above juridical positivism and formalism.[35] He asked that canonists see in the church "the society of the Spirit."[36]

The process of canonical education urgently needs a new design to make it correspond to its newly clarified identity. In the words of the Vatican Council, "in the exposition of canon law...attention must be paid to the mystery of the church." It is to be taught "in the light of faith" and "renewed by a lively contact with the mystery of Christ and salvation history."[37] This theological context is as vital to advanced studies in Canon Law as it is to its introductory investigation. These theological understandings are more than prerequisites for the study of Canon Law, like the knowledge of Greek and Hebrew in preparation for biblical studies. They are integral to the proper perception of what Canon Law is and does. They must suffuse its study. Pope Paul VI had this vision:

> Today it is impossible to carry out studies in canon law without a thorough theological training. The close relationship between canon law and theology is raised, therefore, with urgency.[38]

> Today there is necessary a theology of law which takes up everything that divine revelation says about the mystery of the church. In the various aspects in which are expressed the person and the organization of the church, the action of the Spirit, secret yet outwardly manifest, is present: and this action must constitute the object of your reflection.[39]

The canonist, Paul VI added, is obliged "to search deeper in sacred scripture and theology for the reasons for his own teaching." Canon Law is to be derived "from the very essence of the church of God, for whom the new and original law, that of the gospel, is love."[40]

Canon Law is truly a ministry within the church, and preparation for it must be appropriate for a church ministry both in content and in method.

JESUS ON THE HAZARDS OF THE MINISTRY

Every canonist should begin each work week by reading the entire twenty-third chapter of Matthew's gospel. It contains Jesus' angry denunciation of the scribes and Pharisees. It is a bitter litany of scorn and condemnation. But for the canonist in the church it is a cautionary tale, a sober warning.

> Then Jesus told the crowds and his disciples: "The scribes and Pharisees have succeeded Moses as teachers; therefore do everything and observe everything they tell you. But do not follow their example. Their words are bold but their deeds are few. They bind up heavy loads, hard to carry, to lay on other people's shoulders, while they themselves will not lift a finger to budge them. All their works are performed to be seen. They widen their phylacteries and wear huge tassels. They are fond of places of honor at banquets and the front seats in synagogues, of marks of respect in public and of being called 'Rabbi.' As to you, avoid the title 'Rabbi.' One among you is your teacher, the rest are learners. Do not call anyone on earth your father. Only one is your father, the One in heaven. Avoid being called teachers. Only one is your teacher, the Messiah. The greatest among you will be the one who serves the rest. Whoever exalts himself shall be humbled, but whoever humbles himself shall be exalted.
>
> "Woe to you scribes and Pharisees, you frauds! You shut the doors of the kingdom of God in men's faces, neither entering yourselves nor admitting those who are trying to enter....It is an evil day for you, blind guides!...Woe to you scribes and Pharisees, you frauds! You pay tithes on mint and herbs and seeds while neglecting the weightier matters of the law, justice and mercy and good faith. It is these you should have practiced, without neglecting the others.
>
> "Blind guides! You strain out the gnat and swallow the camel! Woe to you scribes and Pharisees, you frauds! You cleanse the outside of cup and dish, and leave the inside filled with loot and lust! Blind Pharisee! First cleanse the inside of the cup so that its outside may be clean. Woe to you scribes and Pharisees, you frauds! You are like whitewashed tombs, beautiful to look at on the outside, but inside full of

filth and dead people's bones. Thus you present to view a
holy exterior while hypocrisy and evil fill you within....

"O Jerusalem, Jerusalem, murderess of prophets and
stoner of those who were sent to you! How often have I
yearned to gather your children, as a mother bird gathers
her young under her wings, but you refused me."

If the canonist happens to be in a hurry on a given Monday
morning, he or she should at least reflect on the shorter parallel
passage in the eleventh chapter of Luke's gospel, wherein Jesus
singled out "scholars of the law" in particular:

"Woe to you lawyers also! You lay impossible burdens on
people but will not lift a finger to lighten them....Woe to you
lawyers! You have taken away the key of knowledge. You
yourselves have not gained access, yet you have stopped
those who wished to enter!"[41]

All Christians need to remind themselves regularly of what
Jesus said about practicing what they preach, about imposing
burdens on others, about coveting places of honor, about killing
God's prophets, about legal quibbles and wrangles and trivia,
about failures of authenticity and integrity. The warnings are for
all Christ's followers, but canonists especially must attend to
these admonitions.

Canonists, who are teachers and "scholars of the law" in the
Roman Catholic Church, must take these severe sayings to heart
and meditate on them frequently, more so than other believers.
Hypocrisy and legalism are hazards of the ministry today just as
they were in Jesus' time.

AN URGENT AGENDA
FOR THE FUTURE OF THE MINISTRY

THE ARGUMENT OF THIS BOOK is that Canon Law is primarily and principally a ministry within the church. It is a ministry circumscribed by the theology of communion and the concrete realities of congregations of Christ's faithful. It is a ministry devoted to the maintenance of Christian freedom and good order within and among particular and local Catholic churches. Canonical ministry looks forward into the future, searching for the Spirit's guidance.

The book could close with a reiteration of its central argument, or a resume of its principal elements. Instead, in this final section, it will be more fruitful to indicate three agenda items to which canonists must urgently attend. These three are only examples, although very important examples, of what the ministry of Canon Law must address if it is to serve the churches well in the future. The three issues are: 1) a process for revising the canons, 2) provision for diversity of discipline, and 3) canonical creativity.

ONGOING CANONICAL REVISION

The church has long recognized the need for periodic change in its rules of discipline, that is, in its codes of canons,[1] but it has no procedure for their orderly revision. Prior to the twentieth century the church's rules were found in *collections* of canons, rather than *codes* of canons. As changes were needed, papal decrees or canons from councils were simply added to the existing collections or compiled into a new collection, historically subsequent to the previous ones. It was not a tidy system, but there was always room for change.

When the 1917 *Code* went into effect Pope Benedict XV, who promulgated that first codification, made very specific provision for its amendment:

> When in the course of time the good of the universal church calls for a new general decree...after the decree is approved by the Pontiff, it shall be given to the Sacred Congregation of the Council [which had been created to interpret the canons of the Council of Trent], which shall reduce the decision of the decree to a canon or canons. If the decree differs from a prescription of the Code, the Council will indicate for which law of the Code the new law will substitute; if the decree treats of something about which the Code is silent, the Council will establish where the new canon or canons will be inserted into the Code, repeating the number of the preceding canon with *bis, ter,* etc.,...lest the numerical series be disturbed in any way.[2]

This carefully crafted and detailed provision for keeping the *Code* up to date was never used.[3] Rather than make changes in the canons, the popes and the agencies of the Roman Curia created supplemental rules outside the *Code.* This caused the *Code* itself to become outdated, and was one of the reasons that Pope John XXIII called for its *aggiornamento* (updating) in 1959.

The preface to the 1983 *Code* also acknowledged that there would be need for changes:

> When on account of the excessively swift changes in contemporary society certain elements of the present law become less perfect and again require a new *recognitio* (reunderstanding), the church is endowed with such a wealth of

resources that...it will be able readily to undertake the renewal of the laws of its life.[4]

But this time there was no procedure suggested by which to make the required changes in the canons.

The 1990 *Code of Canon of the Eastern Churches* also contained a reference to the need for changes, although this time for ecumenical reasons:

> It is necessary that the canons of the code of the Eastern Catholic churches have the same firmness as the laws of the code of Canon Law of the Latin Church; that is, they will be in force until abrogated or changed by the supreme authority of the Church for a just cause, of which causes full communion of all of the Eastern Churches with the Catholic Church is indeed the most serious.[5]

Again, no process was proposed to carry out needed revisions of the canons.

Even while acknowledging that Canon Law, like all systems of rules, is mutable and will in fact change, the supreme legislative authority provides no way to initiate changes in the church's universal canons. This creates a false impression of permanence or timelessness, a sense that the present rules are perfect and beyond any need for modification or improvement. And this in turn leads to canonical sclerosis. The canons calcify, and with them the canonical ministry. Both tend to decline into formalism, and become anachronistic and increasingly irrelevant. It happened in the decades after the 1917 *Code,* and it is happening again.

The other result, namely the proliferation of supplemental rules outside the *Code,* is also occurring again. The Roman Curia spews out a steady stream of documents containing new norms.[6] The effect is to encumber and obscure the canons with various executive "instructions" on how the rules are to be understood and applied, rather than to permit the updating and modification of the canons themselves.

There is no question that the canonical system, like any other, needs stability; *stabilitas legis* is indeed a value. The churches deserve firm and predictable rules by which to live. But the churches are living and active human communities, led by the Spirit of God. They grow and change, and they require an orderly process for amending, improving, and updating the rules according to which they live.

Even more important than the need for an ordinary, orderly way of amending the canons, is that the procedure be participative. The present practice by which the pope, acting as sole and supreme legislator, can and does take unilateral action, without consultation of the College of Bishops, to change universal laws,[7] is a scandalous manifestation of absolute papal authority. This practice profoundly contradicts the church's own theological identity. It flies in the face of the synodal and conciliar patterns for rule-making which have been the revered and preferred tradition in the church since the "Council of Jerusalem" in Acts 15.[8]

Both the Second Vatican Council and the *Codes* affirm that the College of Bishops also possesses supreme and full power over the universal church along with the pope.[9] One form of that authority is legislative. But there is presently no practical way for the college to exercise its legitimate lawmaking power. The College of Bishops can change canonical rules when acting in an ecumenical council,[10] but such councils are rare, cumbersome, and extremely expensive.

The College of Bishops should collaborate with the pope in revising canonical rules in the context of episcopal synods. The synodal structure already exists, and, when it meets in general session it is broadly representative of the entire college. However, at present episcopal synods are consultative gatherings, purely advisory to the pope and completely controlled by him.[11] But synods can act deliberatively, if and when the pope gives them that power.[12] The popes have not entrusted the synods with issues to decide formally since they first began meeting in 1967. The result of a synod's deliberations would still require papal ratification in order to have binding force, so if and when they were given rule-making authority there would be no threat to papal primacy.

The structure of synods should be altered to make them more effective instruments of collegial governance, but even under the present rules there is nothing to prevent episcopal synods from meeting in legislative sessions. They could regularly consider prepared amendments to the canons or substitutions for them, and in this way, in collaboration with the pope, keep the *Code* current.

The need for a reasonable legislative process is urgent.

DIVERSITY OF DISCIPLINE

Regional diversity of discipline within particular and local churches of the Catholic communion has been a reality for many centuries. Indeed, it has been the persistent pattern of church life from the very beginning. The great canonical collections of the past both revealed that diversity and helped to keep it harmonious.[13] The exercise of papal authority in a centralizing direction has gradually restricted the diversity. The twentieth-century universal codifications of uniform discipline are real innovations within the rich Catholic tradition. Compare this present trend toward uniformity with times past.

The New Testament churches bridged the gap between Jewish and Gentile practices. This was the cause of tension between Peter and Paul, the dispute which was settled in the "Council of Jerusalem."[14] In those first decades these churches also made themselves at home in both Semitic and Greco-Roman cultures. The diversity of their internal ministries is undisputed.[15]

The "church of the empire" (after the fourth century) was far from uniform, even after it had the support of Roman authority and law. Its local communities grew and thrived among all of the various peoples around the Mediterranean basin who were subjects of that imperial authority. The differences in their practices were debated and resolved in the earliest church councils.

Throughout the fifth to eighth centuries the Christian movement encountered and evangelized the peoples who invaded the crumbling empire or lived on its outer fringes. The churches which took root among the Franks, Visigoths, Vandals, Lombards, and Celts all assumed elements from those cultures and were likewise influenced by them.

The later European missionary efforts of the ninth to eleventh centuries, which reached the Polish and Slavic peoples, the Magyars, Bohemians, and Scandinavians, established local churches which incorporated customs and practices of these peoples. Sometimes there were disputes about which "pagan" practices could be reconciled with the Christian faith, but settlements were reached and the communities were accepted in communion.

The missionary efforts of the sixteenth and seventeenth centuries attempted to found churches in the "new worlds" of Africa, America, and Asia. In some places, for example, China, Japan, and India, these heroic efforts were frustrated by the inability or unwillingness to adapt to the cultures and languages of the indigenous peoples. In other places, for example, Central and South America, the Philippines, Goa, the new churches thrived, but often in dominantly European modalities.

At the outset of the twenty-first century, regional Catholic churches all over the earth recognize themselves as integral components of a "world church." They are conscious of the need "to inculturate," to relate reciprocally to their various cultures. They know that they must make the gospel incarnate in their own culture while at the same time introducing the people around them, together with their culture, into their own communities.[16]

Diversity of discipline is a fact of the history and reality of the churches. The variety of practices went much deeper than mere differences in liturgical vestments or church architecture. It included different ways of baptizing and anointing, different forms of receiving holy communion, clerical marriage and clerical celibacy, election of bishops versus appointment of bishops, permanent pastors and temporary ones, personal parishes as well as territorial ones. It is clear that a considerable diversity of discipline among the churches was respected from the beginnings of the Christian tradition.

Beyond recognizing the fact of diversity and its full legitimacy, inculturation calls for the ability to continue to adapt church practices so that they are meaningful to people in particular places and times, so that the people see them as their own and not as something foreign to them. Of course, the adaptations to various cultures must always be in keeping with the common faith and not jeopardize the strong bonds of communion. However, genuine inculturation demands a healthy diversity of practice.

The salient question is, How is this regional diversity of discipline to develop? How can it be fostered and monitored? The answer lies in the church's tradition of conciliar structures.

During the early centuries a rich variety of regional disciplinary practices was established and maintained through regional synods, for example, in North Africa, in southern France, in central Spain,[17] and by the established synods of the patriarchal churches: Antioch, Alexandria, Jerusalem, and Constantinople. These decisional and policy-making bodies exercised authority in their regions both before and after papal primacy was acknowledged and papal decretal activity became prevalent.

Regional councils functioned throughout the Merovingian (sixth and seventh centuries) and the Carolingian (eighth and ninth centuries) periods. This pattern of regional conciliar action evolved into the system of provincial and metropolitan councils which continued throughout the Middle Ages. As papal authority waxed in modern times, regional conciliar activity waned.[18] Roman authority became stronger and more centralized, and it gradually resisted and broke down the pattern of conciliar functioning.

The decrees of the popes and the directives of their curial congregations, however, often recognized and respected regional differences. At their best they safeguarded regional and ritual traditions, and even encouraged local adaptations. However, their tendency, over the centuries, was toward centralization, to the detriment of regional decision-making.

Roman authorities in the twentieth century insisted on control over regional decisions. Plenary councils, for all the dioceses whose bishops belong to the same conference, cannot be held without the prior permission of the Apostolic See, and the norms which those councils decide upon cannot be promulgated until the Holy See has approved them.[19] The result of these restrictions is that such councils no longer occur. Parallel limitations severely confine the rule-making activity of episcopal conferences.[20] The pre-promulgation review *(recognitio)* of conference decisions by the Apostolic See[21] retards rule-making activity and obstructs the healthy processes of innovation and adaptation.

This effective suppression of regional self-determination leaves the universal norms of the codes in exclusive control. The whole process is centripetal. It not only restricts legislative power to the central authority, but it persistently compels uniformity of practice to the detriment of cultural or pastoral adaptation.

In sum, uniform universal legislation, epitomized in the canonical codes of the twentieth century and enforced by the supreme central authority, has replaced the long tradition of regional adaptation. The postconciliar promise of a return to collegiality and subsidiary function has failed to materialize. As a result, at present in the Roman Catholic communion the means for regional self-regulation and pastoral adaptation are woefully inadequate.

One possible structure for the achievement of some region-alized church discipline is the episcopal synod. Since the Second Vatican Council some regional episcopal synods have been held, for example, for Africa, for Europe, for America, and for Asia,[22] but these were purely consultative with no regulative results. Such synods could be asked to exercise regulatory responsibilities for their regions,[23] but such authority has not yet been given to them.

It must be noted that the unity of the entire Catholic communion is essential. But it is a unity in essentials *(in necesariis)*, and freedom is to be encouraged in all other matters, including various forms of discipline *(in variis formis...disciplinae)*.[24] Diversity is nearly as high a value as unity. Moreover, the papal office is not the only one responsible for the church's unity. It is the responsibility of every bishop, every local congregation, every single one of the Christian faithful.[25] Ultimately, the Holy Spirit is the guardian of the church's unity as well as the impetus behind its diversity.

Instant worldwide communications and accelerated travel give rise to both complications and opportunities regarding the diversity of disciplinary practices. Everyone has almost immediate access to information about whatever practice occurs in any regional church. But this knowledge is not detrimental to the unity of the church. Great cultural differences still exist, despite enhanced communications. Modern media make it easier to read the "vital signs" of the local churches; they show forth the vigor of different traditions. Shared knowledge is a source of further creative adaptation, that is, it is a force for freedom in local churches, rather than an excuse for needless uniformity or homogenization.

CANONICAL CREATIVITY

Canonists are not always characterized as imaginative. They are usually perceived as persons who interpret and apply the church's rules in routine and predictable ways. Stability and evenhandedness are commendable virtues, but creativity and imagination will also be needed for this ministry in the future.

The pastoral concerns for divorced and remarried Catholics in North America provide two examples of canonical creativity, one past and one ahead.

First, an example from the recent past. Soon after the conclusion of the Second Vatican Council, canonists and bishops in the United States, impelled by the spiritual energy and pastoral enthusiasm of that time, sought and secured a set of changes in the marriage annulment process for their diocesan tribunals. Members of the Canon Law Society of America and the Bishop's Committee for Canonical Affairs developed a set of modified procedural norms designed to expedite the adjudication of marriage nullity petitions.

The U.S. conference of bishops proposed the norms to Pope Paul VI in 1969, and, after some alterations, he approved them in 1970. Notable among the derogations from the general law of the 1917 *Code* were the ability to have cases decided by a single judge (rather than the collegiate panel of three judges), and the elimination of the need to have the decisions reviewed by an appellate tribunal.[26]

These "streamlined" procedures coincided with the emergence of the "psychological grounds" for marriage nullity petitions, that is, the various developmental problems or personality disorders which might cause a person's matrimonial consent to be defective. Diocesan bishops and their canonists also improved their marriage tribunals in the same period, enlarging their personnel and expanding their financial resources.

The results were dramatic. In 1968 American tribunals decided 442 "formal cases," in 1978 they decided 27,737.[27] A virtual explosion of annulments had occurred. In 1985, after the special "American Norms" had expired and the canons of the 1983 *Code* replaced them, the number of decisions was 44,170. In 1995 the number was 41,506.[28]

This canonical initiative, the fruit of genuine imagination and great industry, revolutionized the ministry to the divorced and remarried Catholics in the United States. Hundreds of thousands of Christ's faithful have returned to full sacramental communion in their church as a result. Still, it is only fair to say that the number of those who were reached and reconciled by this canonical process represents a small fraction of those Catholics whose lives have been touched by the tragedy of divorce in the United States. This creative response, which is entirely deserving of commendation and praise, remains pastorally inadequate.

Now, an example for the future. What is needed is a more comprehensive vision of the pastoral situation of those in irregular marriages and a more flexible response to them.

First of all, the Christian tradition holds that contentious controversies are to be avoided, not encouraged. As the *Codes* state:

> All the Christian faithful and especially bishops are to strive diligently to avoid litigation among the people of God as much as possible, with due regard for justice, and to resolve litigation peacefully as soon as possible.[29]

The canon reflects an evangelical imperative. Jesus' own admonition to avoid litigation rings down the centuries and resounds in this canon of the *Codes:*

> Lose no time; settle with your opponent while on your way to court with him. (Mt 5, 25)

> When you are going with your opponent to appear before a magistrate, try to settle with him on the way lest he turn you over to the judge. (Lk 12, 58)

These sayings of Jesus are more than prudent advice or folk wisdom. They are closely related to the radical gospel values of peace, forgiveness, and reconciliation.[30]

In the light of Jesus' teaching on avoiding litigation it seems obvious that the contentious judicial process to determine the status of persons is inappropriate, to say the least. Even when the judicial process of annulment is not actually adversarial (i.e., is noncontested) it is an inadequate and inappropriate way to deal with the immense pastoral problem of divorced and remarried Catholics for other reasons.

The tribunal process is inadequate because it is unavailable in many parts of the world. Even where good, functioning tribunals do exist, the procedure is cumbersome, distasteful, removed from the local community, and sometimes expensive. The annulment procedure often gives rise to serious misunderstandings, for example, that a marriage never existed, that the children are illegitimate, or even scandal, for example, when long-term or multiple marriages are declared invalid.

The process frequently pursues and resolves the wrong question. An ancient Roman law procedure for the determination of the *status personarum,* slave or free, citizen or foreigner, is used by the church to determine whether a person is bound by marriage or is free to marry. But very often divorced Catholics come to ask, not the declaration of their free status, but to be reconciled to the church. They seek God's forgiveness and a return to full sacramental communion. They do not seek another decision about the validity of their former marriage; they have already endured a civil divorce proceeding. They feel rejected and alienated from their community of faith. They seek acceptance, support, mercy, and love from and within their Christian community. What is needed, most of the time, is not a judicial process to ascertain the status of persons, but a process of ecclesial reconciliation that leads to full eucharistic communion.

Local and particular churches should adopt a more appropriate and comprehensive course of action to address this immense pastoral problem. It should be a multifaceted and flexible approach, one that offers alternative avenues.

When all efforts to reconcile a couple have failed and the breakdown of the marriage relationship is complete and final, pastoral watchfulness and discernment come into play. If and when one of the parties approaches the local church or can be contacted by it, before or after attempting a second marriage, a pastoral agent[31] intervenes to assist that person to explore the various avenues to grace and ecclesial reconciliation. This pastoral minister listens intently to the story of the person's faith, marriage, its failure, as well as the story of a remarriage, if one has occurred. Then the pastoral minister helps the person (or couple), who exercise the virtue of *epikeia,* to choose a course of action which will lead them to repentance, conversion, and reconciliation with God and with the local church.

Among the options which they might embrace are one or more of the following:

- a process of spiritual formation and guidance, perhaps a group process similar to that for the Christian Initiation of Adults, a sort of modern "order of penitents" engaged in a gradual process of reconciliation;
- access to the sacraments of penance and Eucharist after a careful discernment in which of all of the relevant issues are considered, including responsibilities for previous marriage and children, personal repentance and conversion, prospects for the present union, possible scandal, and involvement in church life; after such a guided reflection

the couple once again approach the sacraments of forgiveness and full communion;

- a tolerated civil marriage: a very widespread phenomenon which is recognized as a public "commitment to a properly defined and probably stable state of life,"[32] one contracted "for ideological or practical reasons," and quite different from an "obstinate persistence in manifest grave sin," the canonical criterion for exclusion from holy communion;[33]
- a nonsacramental and penitential recognition of a second union; a prayerful and somber acknowledgment by the community of faith of the tragic outcome of the first union and a loving and hope-filled pledge of support for the present one, in no way to be confused with the celebration of a pristine sacramental covenant;
- affiliation with another local church (i.e., parish); when the situation might give rise to *admiratio* or scandal in one parish or neighborhood, then enrollment elsewhere might be advisable;
- in a mixed marriage, possible recourse to another church or ecclesial communion; both the couple and their marital situation might be better received in the church of the non-Catholic party if that party is of firm faith and such a transfer of affiliation seems mutually acceptable;
- when certain marriages require formal judicial determination, for reasons of personal conscience or public propriety, and that process is realistically available, then the tribunal should carry out its proper function of adjudication, so that justice is served.[34]

This multioption pastoral strategy is operative even now in many particular and local churches, for instance, at St. Mary's on Main Street, with the approval of the pastors of those churches. But in many places this pastoral plan is in competition with the litigious alternative, the judicial annulment process. In such areas the tribunal's productive activity may actually impede more effective and desirable pastoral action.

When the tribunal is held out as the only official and approved means of reconciliation for the divorced and remarried, then it stands in the way of other legitimate and perhaps preferable forms of pastoral assistance. When bishops and priests encourage petitions for nullity of marriages, and the courts actually grant as many of them as possible, then the tribunal "occupies the field." Its resources and prestige overshadow all other approaches to reconciliation. An exclusive focus on the juridical forum diverts attention, personnel, and resources from more supple and suitable forms of pastoral assistance.

A more balanced and flexible pastoral plan for the reconciliation of the divorced and remarried, one which actively discouraged contentious litigation among the people of God and favored the peaceful resolution of their differences, would be a welcome exercise of canonical creativity.

In Conclusion

Canon Law is an organically developing ministry, not a closed system of laws. It is a theologically driven project of church leadership that strives to maintain both Christian freedom and good order, not a fixed set of uniform rules woodenly applied.

Without the ability to update its rules in an ongoing and orderly manner, the ministry of Canon Law atrophies. Without the ability to adapt its norms to communities in different cultures, the ministry cannot advance the mission of the churches. Without creativity and imagination, the ministry will stiffen into formalism.

The ministry of Canon Law serves local churches, churches which are living and growing, churches enlivened and led by the Holy Spirit.

The local church is a garden and the minister of Canon Law the gardener. Plants have constant basic needs: light, water, soil. But they are always changing. A devoted gardener attends to the plants and grounds in season and out of season: planning, planting, tending, harvesting, clearing, and then beginning again.

Local churches, like gardens, are works in progress, always becoming. The Holy Spirit enlivens and renews them. An attentive and robust canonical ministry can help them to thrive and flourish.

NOTES

1. THE DEBATE ABOUT THE NATURE OF CANON LAW

1. For references, confer G. Caprile, *Il concilio Vaticano II, Periodo primo* (Rome, 1968), 197, 239, 241–44, 246, 248–50, 253, 257, 280, 555.

2. R. Sohm, *Kirchenrecht, I: die geschichtlichen Grundlagen* (Leipzig, 1892; Berlin, 1970), 2.

3. Ibid., 700.

4. Y. Congar, "Rudolph Sohm nous interroge encore," *Rev. Sci. Phil. Theol.* 57(1973): 263–94.

5. The Letter to the Philippians, *Letters and Papers from Prison, Letter from a Birmingham Jail.*

6. These viewpoints or schools of thought are described, with variations, by several contemporary authors: Eugenio Corecco, Péter Erdö, Libero Geroso, Julián Herranz, Ann Jacobs, Ladislas Örsy, Carlo Redaelli, Myriam Wijlens. Some of the categories are common parlance in the debate, others are innovations. The names associated with the "schools" are given below in alphabetical order, not in the order of importance, influence, or chronological sequence.

7. Names linked with this school of thought are Pietro d'Avack, Vincenzo del Giudice, Pio Fedele, Orio Giacchi, Pietro Gismondi.

8. Some authors associated with this position are Juan Arrieta, Maria Blanco, Arturo Cattaneo, Juan Fornés, Alberto de la Hera, Javier Hervada, Pedro Lombardía, Pedro Viladrich.

9. *Rationis ordinatio ad bonum commune, ab eo qui curam communitatem habet, promulgata.* Summa Theologiae, I–II, 90, 4.

10. The proponents of this view, associated with the faculty of Canon Law at the University of Munich, include Winfried Aymans, Eugenio Corecco, Klaus Mörsdorf, Antonio Rouco Varela, Remigiusz Sobanski.

11. Names associated with this view, most of whom taught in the faculty of Canon Law at the Gregorian University and assisted in the Roman Curia, include Wilhelm Bertrams, Raimondo Bidagor, Piero Bonnet.

12. Teodoro Jiménez-Urresti, Peter Huizing, and Knut Walf are the persons most consistently linked to this viewpoint. It is referred to as the Concilium Project because Canon Law's relativized relationship to theology was enunciated in the first canonical issue of the journal *Concilium* in 1965.

13. Ladislas Örsy and Myriam Wijlens are the names most closely associated with this viewpoint and its unique focus on values.

14. John Paul II, Apost. Const. *Sacrae disciplinae leges,* January 25, 1983. This document of promulgation is printed in the front of every edition of the *Code of Canon Law.*

15. Francesco Coccopalmerio, Velasio De Paolis, Péter Erdö, Gianfranco Ghirlanda, and Aldolpho Longhitano are some of the names associated with this institutional vision of Canon Law.

2. About Roots and Names and History

1. Which were, in other words, the proscriptions of Leviticus 17 and 18 for aliens living in Israel.

2. For example, the sharing of gifts by many persons subsided as the presider gradually assumed all the roles, speaking in tongues ceased, and women no longer kept silent in the assemblies.

3. For example, the observance of the Levitical dietary regulations.

4. The 1990 *Code of Canons of the Eastern Churches (Codex Canonum Ecclesiarum Orientalium)* happily avoided this confusing use of the English word *law.*

3. A VISION OF CHURCH: THE THEOLOGICAL
CONTEXT FOR THE MINISTRY

1. This "*communio* ecclesiology" is drawn from and dependent upon the writings of Yves Congar, Ludwig von Hertling, Jerome Hamer, Karl Rahner, Severino Dianich, Giuseppe Colombo, Walter Kasper, Edward Schillebeeckx, Michael Fahey, Edward Kilmartin, Jean-Marie Tillard, Hervé Legrand, and Joseph Komonchak.

2. *...in quibus et ex quibus una et unica ecclesia catholica existit* (*LG* 23).

3. *SC* 51, *DV* 21, *AG* 9.

4. *...participatio actuosa* (*SC* 48).

5. E.g., *LG* 48, *AA* 3, *AG* 4, *CD* 11, *GS* 21 and 43.

6. Jn 7, 37–39; 2 Cor 3, 6; Acts 1, 8.

7. Jn 14, 16–17, and 26; Jn 15, 26; Mt 10, 19–20; Acts 1, 1–2; 1 Cor 2, 10–13.

8. 1 Cor 12, 7–11; Eph 4.

9. Rom 8, 26–27; Jn 16, 7.

10. Jn 20, 21–23.

11. Acts 13, 2–4; 15, 28–29; 16, 6–8; Rom 8, 14.

12. 2 Cor 13, 13; 1 Cor 12, 13.

13. 2 Cor 3, 17; Gal 4 and 5; Rom 8, 2; 1 Thes 5, 19–21.

14. 1 Cor 12, 4–11; *LG* 12.

15. *Non...de vago quodam affectu, sed de realitate organica*; *Nota praevia*, 2, to *LG*. Emphasis in original.

16. *LG* 7 and 13.

17. *koinonia*; Acts 2, 42.

18. *koinonia pneumatos*; Phil 2, 1.

19. Rom 15, 26; 2 Cor 9, 13.

20. *LG* 3, 7, 11, *UR* 2, 15, 22, *AG* 39, *AA* 8, *PO* 6.

21. "Contribution" is another meaning of *koinonia*; Rom 15, 26; 2 Cor 9, 13.

22. *...in quibus et ex quibus...existit*; *LG* 23.

23. *LG* 18–24, *CD* 4–7, *PO* 7, 15.

24. These elements are stated in *LG* 14. This rich theological description of full communion is greatly attenuated in its canonical restatements. See *CIC* 205 and *CCEO* 8.

25. These factors are present in *LG* 15.

26. These elements are specified in *UR* 3.

27. Lk 22, 20; 1 Cor 11, 25.

28. *LG* 13, in which the Greek text of Acts 2, 42, is cited.

29. 1 Pt 2, 9; *SC* 14.

30. *Justice in the World*, statement of the Synod of Bishops, November 30, 1971. *AAS* 63 (1971): 923–42; *Proclaiming Justice and Peace*, ed. M. Walsh and B. Davies (Mystic, Conn.: Twenty-Third Publications, 1991), 268–83.

31. 1 Cor 12, 12 and 27; cf. also Eph 1, 6.

32. Eph 1, 22–23; 6, 23.

33. *GS* 45; cf. also *LG* 9 and *SC* 5.

34. The church is often called the "primordial" or "root sacrament."

35. The salvific plan is called in Greek, *mysterion*; in Latin, *sacramentum*.

36. *LG* 8; confer also *LG* 15 and *GS* 43 for affirmations of sinfulness and need for renewal.

37. Rom 15, 26–28; 1 Cor 16, 1–2.

38. Confer: *AD* 11, *GS* 39, *NA* 1.

39. *LG* 20, 21, 24; *CD* 2; *DV* 8.

40. *paratheke*; 1 Tm 6, 20; 2 Tm 1, 14.

41. *didaskalia*; 1 Tm 1, 10; 2 Tm 4, 3.

42. *charisma*; 1 Tm 4, 13; 2 Tm 1, 6.

4. CHURCHES IN PLACE: THE SITUATIONAL CONTEXT FOR THE MINISTRY

1. Jas 1, 25; 2, 12.

2. 2 Cor 8, 13–15; see all of chaps. 8 and 9 and 1 Cor 16, 1–4.

3. *CIC*, c. 755.1; *CCEO*, c. 902; confer the Decree on Ecumenism (*UR*).

4. Declaration on the Relationship of the Church to Non Christian Religions (*NA*).

5. Declaration on Religious Freedom (*DH*).

6. *CIC*, c. 535; *CCEO*, c. 296. Indeed, parish histories should be an integral part of the required parish archives.

7. *Quadragesimo anno*, Encyclical Letter on the Fortieth Anniversary of *Rerum novarum*, May 15, 1931; *AAS* 23 (1931): 177–228; *Proclaiming Justice and Peace*, 41–80.

8. Encyclical Letter on a Reevaluation of the Social Question, May 15, 1961; *AAS* 53 (1961): 401–64; *Proclaiming Justice and Peace*, 81–124.

9. *Centesimus annus,* Encyclical Letter on the One Hundredth Anniversary of *Rerum novarum,* May 1, 1991; *AAS* 83 (1991): 854; *Proclaiming Justice and Peace,* 432–78.

10. In addresses by Pope Pius XII on February 20, 1946 (*AAS* 38 [1946]: 145), and by Pope Paul VI on October 27, 1969 (*AAS* 61 [1969]: 729).

11. Principle No. 5, quoted in the Preface to the 1983 *Code of Canon Law;* for the full text of the principle of revision, see *Communicationes* 1 (1969): 80–82.

12. *Sollicitudo rei socialis,* Encyclical Letter on Social Concerns, December 30, 1987; *AAS* 80 (1988): 513–86; *Proclaiming Justice and Peace,* 392–431.

5. FREEDOM IN THE CHURCH: FIRST FOCUS OF THE MINISTRY OF THE CANONIST

1. See his extended allegory in Gal 4, 21–31.

2. Those found, in the same order, in Lv 17 and 18.

3. K. Rahner, *Concern for the Church (Theological Investigations XX)* (New York: Crossroad, 1981), 63.

4. "The gospel announces and proclaims the liberty of God's children, rejects every slavery as ultimately resulting from sin, and reverently respects the dignity of conscience and its free decision, continually teaches that all human talents should be devoted to God's service and the wellbeing of women and men, and commends all to the love of all" (*GS* 41).

5. That is, in which conscience is seen as a faculty of the person rather than being identified with the person.

6. *Communicationes* 1 (1969): 79–80, principle n. 3, on ways of promoting pastoral care. (The paragraph on discretion was omitted when the principles were published in the preface of the 1983 *Code.*)

7. Pope Paul VI, *Paenitemini,* February 17, 1966, *AAS* 58 (1966): 179–98; English translation of the same date published in brochure form by the National Catholic Welfare Conference; also in *Documents on the Liturgy, 1963–1979,* ed. T. O'Brien (Collegeville, Minn.: Liturgical Press, 1982), 935–43.

8. Address, February 4, 1977; *AAS* 69 (1977): 151; *The Pope Speaks* 22 (1977): 178.

9. See note 7 above.

10. *Digitus Paternae dexterae*, from the hymn at Vespers on Pentecost, *Veni, Creator Spiritus*.

11. 1 Cor 12, 3; cf. also 1 Jn 4, 2-3.

12. A similar argument, made by Gamaliel the Pharisee, "a teacher of the law highly regarded by all the people," convinced the Sanhedrin to dismiss the apostles: "If their purpose or activity is human in its origins, it will destroy itself. If, on the other hand, it comes from God, you will not be able to destroy them without fighting God himself" (Acts 5, 34-39).

13. Mt 16, 3; Lk 12, 56.

14. Confer also *UR* 4.

15. Apostolic letter *Octagesimo adveniens*, May 14, 1971, par. 4; *AAS* 63 (1971): 1103; *Proclaiming Justice and Peace*, 248.

16. October 26, 1974, par. 6; *Origins* 4:20 (November 7, 1974): 307.

17. *CIC* 208-23, *CCEO* 10-26.

18. The circumstances of this omission may be found in the *Proceedings of the Canon Law Society of America* 58 (1996): 138.

19. For example, the canons on the rights and duties of the Christian faithful, the role of pastors, the teaching function of the church, the sacramental life, the church's mission and educational responsibilities, and the temporal goods of the churches.

20. Paul VI, Apostolic Exhortation *Evangelii nuntiandi*, December 8, 1975, 63; *AAS* 68 (1976): 53-54; *Proclaiming Justice and Peace*, 310.

21. Ibid., 63.1; p. 310.

22. Extraordinary Synod of 1985, Final Report, II, D, 4; *Origins* 15:27 (December 19, 1985): 450.

23. John Paul II, Encyclical *Redemptoris missio*, December 7, 1990, 52; *AAS* 83 (1991): 299-302; *Origins* 20:34 (January 31, 1991): 556. The extensive treatment of inculturation in the encyclical (nos. 52-54) drew upon the pope's earlier writings and speeches, most notably his Apostolic Constitution *Catchesi tradendae*, October 16, 1979, 53; *Origins* 9:21 (November 8, 1979): 344; *AAS* 71 (1979): 1319-20, his Encyclical *Slavorum apostoli*, June 2, 1985, *AAS* 77 (1985): 802ff.; *Origins* 15:8 (July 18, 1985): 121-22, and his talks to the bishops of Zaire, Kenya, India, and Colombia (cited in note 88 of *Redemptoris missio*).

24. *Origins* 28:2 (May 28, 1998): 19, 20, 25, 27. In the Synod, reference was made to the church's "unity in diversity" and to the expression *"in essentialibus unitas, in accedentalibus libertas, in omnibus caritas."*
25. Synod Secretariat, Working Paper for the Synod of Asian Bishops, 50; *Origins* 27:38 (March 12, 1998): 649–50.
26. Confer also *DH* 14.

6. GOOD ORDER IN THE CHURCH: SECOND FOCUS OF THE CANONICAL MINISTRY

1. Confer Jn 3, 6–8, 1 Thes 5, 19–22.
2. *euskamonos kai kata taxin*, 1 Cor 14, 40; for the same usage of *taxin*, good order, see Col 2, 5.
3. Mk 10, 42–45; parallel: Mt 20, 25–28.
4. One translation of the words *diakonia, ministerium*, and ministry.
5. 1 Cor 1, 3; see also 1 Thes 2 and 1 Cor 9.
6. For instance, the multivolume *Handbook of Church History*, ed. H. Jedin and J. Dolan (New York: Seabury, 1965ff.).
7. For example, Theodosius II (408–50) and Justinian (527–65).
8. For example, *ius, potestas, auctoritas, ordo, decretum, forum, jurisdictio, dioecesis.*
9. Named for the practice of an emperor or king investing a bishop or abbot with the symbols of his office, the pastoral staff and ring, thus making him both a prelate of the church and a vassal of the king.
10. Cc. 129 and 274 of the 1983 *Code*; c. 118 of the 1917 *Code*.
11. These papal powers are asserted in canons 331 and 333 of the 1983 *Code*, canons 43 and 45 of the 1990 *CCEO*, and in the constitution *Pastor aeternus* of Vatican I, and *LG* 22 of Vatican II.
12. The council text cites these New Testament passages: Acts 1, 17 and 25; 21, 19; Rom 11, 13; 1 Tm 1, 12.
13. See Lk 22, 26–27; *LG* 27.
14. Apostolic constitution *Sacrae disciplinae leges*, January 25, 1983, placed in front of all editions of the 1983 *Code*. In fact, the new *Code* honors the teaching largely by its silence. The only explicit reference to authority as service, among the hundreds of times that power and authority are mentioned, occurs in regard to superiors of religious institutes (c. 618).

15. From the Greek words, *ieros* (holy) and *arche* (rule).

16. Hilduin of Saint-Denis, writing in the ninth century, said that Dionysius had been the bishop of Paris (!). *The Complete Works* (see following footnote, pp. 21–22).

17. Abbreviated *CH*. P. Rorem, *Pseudo-Dionysius: A Commentary on the Texts and an Introduction to Their Influence* (New York: Oxford University Press, 1993); *Pseudo-Dionysius the Areopagite: The Complete Works*, trans. C. Luibhed, ed. P. Rorem (New York: Paulist Press, 1987),143–91.

18. Abbreviated *EH*. D. Rutledge, *Cosmic Theology; The Ecclesiastical Hierarchy of Pseudo-Dioysius, An Introduction* (Staten Island, N.Y.: Alba House, 1965); Pseudo-Dionysius the Areopagite, *The Ecclesiastical Hierarchy*, trans. T. Campbell (Washington, D.C.: University Press of America, 1981).

19. Once it is used in a title (Part II of Book II), and five times in the section on administrative recourse (cc. 1732–39). The terms are used very sparingly in the 1990 *CCEO*, e.g., cc. 27, 147, 307, 309, 322, 916.

20. This assertion of equality as a starting point is the diametric opposite of that which described the church as a "perfect society of unequals" (*societas perfecta inaequalium*). Cf. A. Ottaviani, *Institutiones Iuris Publici Ecclesiastici*, 3rd ed. (Roma: Typis Polyglot. Vaticanis, 1947), n. 112.

21. Confer *LG* 9–13 for an authoritative elaboration of this theme.

22. "Monarchy" comes from the Greek words *monos* and *archein*, meaning "to rule alone." It has sometimes happened that pastors, bishops, and popes have ruled like monarchs, but that is not the normal way that authority as service is to be exercised in the church. Ottaviani, in his expression of *societas perfecta* ecclesiology, openly asserted the monarchical constitution of the church and the monarchical character of the governance of diocesan bishops (op. cit., nn. 211, 221).

23. For a fine summary of the debate, confer J. Beal, "The Exercise of the Power of Governance by Lay People: State of the Question," *Jurist* 55 (1995): 1–92.

24. Religious superiors exercise the power of governance when they administer church property, admit or dismiss members of their institute, erect or suppress provinces and houses, or remove a religious from an ecclesiastical office. Confer *CIC*, cc. 635, 641, 656, 658, 699, 609, 581, 564, 616, 682.

25. Examples: *CIC*, cc. 129.2, 228, 494, 517.2, 618, 636, 1421.2, etc.

26. That is, those in sacred orders are capable (*habiles*) of the power while laypersons can cooperate in its exercise (*cooperari possunt in exercitio potestatis*); *CIC*, c. 129.

27. Beal, "The Exercise of Power," p. 57; also in *Antonianum* 58 (1983): 641, n. 36, and in *Ius Canonicum* 26 (1986): 586–88.

28. *Congregatio Plenaria diebus 20–29 octobris habita*, ed. Pont. Consilium de Legum Textibus Interpretandis (Vatican City: Typis Polyglottis Vaticanis, 1991), 211–12; the votes ranged from 52–9 to 59–2.

29. The expression Paul used in writing to the Corinthians, *kata taxin* (1 Cor 14, 40).

7. CANON LAW AS MINISTRY

1. The source for these estimates is the 1998 membership registration of the Canon Law Society of America, which has sixteen hundred members.

2. This seems to be true even of the increasing number of lay canonists, although many also teach in educational institutions or are affiliated with a personal prelature.

3. In effect, the canonist might think and act like a corporate attorney, and lose sight of the broader ecclesial responsibilities of the ministry. Two parallels: an "attorney at law" is always an "officer of the court" even when representing a client; a bishop engaged in ministerial action represents the church and not simply his own views or interests or those of one group or faction within the diocese.

4. In the second set of gifts, that is, after the first three, apostle, prophet, and teacher, and along with the gifts of miracle worker, healer, assistant, and speaker in tongues (v. 28).

5. Council of Trent, session 22, decree on reform, canon 2 (September 17, 1562); canon 378, 1, 5 of the 1983 *Code*, c. 331, 1, 5 of the 1917 *Code*. (The 1990 *CCEO*, c. 180, calls for a graduate degree or expertise in "some sacred science," whereas the source for the canon, c. 394 of the 1957 motu proprio *Cleri sanctitati*, said in "sacred theology or canon law.")

6. Early Christian art and literature frequently depicted Christ as the helmsman guiding a ship (the church) through stormy seas.

7. 1 Cor 12, 4–7, 12–27.

8. 1 Cor 14, 26 and 40; confer chapter 12 on the sources and coordination of the gifts.

9. Motu proprio *Ministeria quaedam*, August 15, 1972, *AAS* 64 (1972): 529–34; *CLD* 7, 690–95.

10. The absence of biblical expressions in the canons is truly remarkable. It almost appears as though biblical language had been systematically eliminated. Two exceptions in the 1983 *CIC*: 1) canon 762 on preaching cites the prophet Malachi (2, 7) about requiring the word of God from the mouths of priests, and 2) canon 1199 on oaths quotes Jeremiah (4, 2) in saying that oaths are not to be taken except "in truth, in judgment, and in justice." In neither instance is the biblical source mentioned in the official footnotes!

11. Confer *Summa Theologiae*, I, q.1, a. 1. Note that the purpose of theology is to serve the salvation of humankind, not simply to speculate about God.

12. J. Koury demonstrates this in *"Ius Divinum* as a Canonical Problem: On the Interaction of Divine and Ecclesiastical Laws," *Jurist* 53 (1993): 104–31. See also P Erdö, *"Ius Divinum* between Normative Text, Normative Content, and Material Value Structure," *Jurist* 56 (1996): 41–67.

13. In canons 22, 24.1, 1059, 1075.1, 1163.2, 1165.2, 1290, and 1692.2.

14. For instance, it was widely thought that the impediment of consanguinity, which has changed many times in the church's history, was of "divine law" in prohibiting marriages in the first degree of the collateral line, that is, between brother and sister, until Pope Paul VI authorized the granting of a dispensation (January 21, 1977) to permit such a marriage. He declared that impediment was of ecclesiastical law. *CLD* 9:627–28. Similarly, the impediment of impotence is widely regarded as being "of divine law," but now that marriage has been redefined as "a partnership of the whole of life" (*totius vitae consortium*; c. 1055) rather than as a contract whose primary end is the procreation and education of children (1917 *Code*, cc. 1012, 1013), is it not probable that marriages involving a partner who is organically impotent will be permitted, as long as that condition is known and accepted by the other partner?

15. Canons 98.2, 199.1, 748.1, 1249, 1315.1, and 1399.

16. Contrary to the views of the "schools" of Public Ecclesiastical Law and Opus Dei, chapter 1.

17. As the Opus Dei, Munich, and Concilium Project schools affirm; see chapter 1.

18. As both the Concilium Project and the Roman Curia schools assert, chapter 1. The Roman Curia school seems to "over-ontologize" or exaggerate the metaphysical necessity of the church's structures.

19. As the Institutional School holds; see chapter 1. However, there is danger in attributing very much of the basic structure of the church to its Divine Founder. Too many elements have been deemed to be "of divine law," only to be modified or discarded subsequently.

20. Confer John Paul II, Apostolic constitution *Sacrae disciplinae leges* (January 25, 1983) on the purpose of the 1983 *Code; AAS* 75 (1983): xi.

21. Confer the "Public Ecclesiastical Law School" in chapter 1.

22. Confer the "Munich School" in chapter 1. Their substitution of *ordinatio fidei* for *ordinatio rationis* in the definition of Canon Law is helpful to the extent that it indicates Christian faith as the essential context for all canonical regulation, but contrasting the terms can make it appear that faith and reason are somehow in conflict. The canons are rational "orderings" of things related to faith.

23. *CIC* cc. 17, 1608.2, 125.1.

24. *OT* 16.

25. Ibid.

26. *CIC*, cc. 1421.3, 378.1.5; also: vicars general and episcopal (478.1), judicial vicars (1420.4), promotors of justice and defenders of the bond (1435), advocates (1483), and seminary teachers (253.1).

27. Two sets of norms were issued in the twentieth century: Pius XI, Apostolic constitution, *Deus scientiarum Dominus* (May 24, 1931) and the attached *ordinationes* (*AAS* 23 [1931]: 241–84, and John Paul II, Apostolic constitution *Sapientia Christiana*, April 15, 1979, and the Norms of Application (*AAS* 71 [1979]: 469–521), English translation, "On Ecclesiastical Universities and Faculties," published by the USCC in 1979).

28. *SapChris*, arts. 75–77.

29. Norms, arts. 55–57.

30. Norms, art. 57.1.

31. *SapChris*, art. 75.

32. Norms, art. 57.2.

33. Compare art. 29 of the *Deus Scientiarum Dominus* and arts. 26–27 of its *ordinationes* with arts. 75–77 of *Sapientia Christiana* and arts. 55–57 of its Norms.

34. *AAS* 57 (1965): 988, in his allocution of November 20, 1965, charging the Pontifical Council for the Revision of the Code of Canon Law with its post-conciliar task.

35. Address, January 19, 1970; *The Pope Speaks* 15 (1970–71): 74.

36. Ibid. It is ironic that Pope Paul VI did so little to change the course of canonical studies so as to induce the formation of a "new way of thinking" in those who pursue its academic degrees. He changed almost nothing in the programs of canonical studies to facilitate this new outlook. Pope John Paul II states in the introduction to *Sapientia Christiana* that it was composed under Paul VI, but its promulgation was delayed due to his death (in 1978).

37. *OT* 16.

38. Address, September 17, 1973; *Origins* 3 (1973–74): 263.

39. Ibid., 262.

40. Address, January 19, 1970; *loc. cit.*, 73.

41. Lk 11, 46 and 52.

An Urgent Agenda for the Future of the Ministry

1. In the twentieth century: the 1917 *Code of Canon Law*, the 1983 *Code of Canon Law*, and the 1990 *Code of Canons for the Eastern Churches*.

2. *Motu proprio Cum iuris canonici*, September 15, 1917, III; printed in the front of the 1917 *Code*.

3. When Pope Pius XII modified canon 1099 on the canonical form of marriage in 1948, it was noted in the *Code* with an asterisk and a footnote. *Motu proprio Abrogatur alterum*, August 1, 1948.

4. Final paragraph of the unsigned preface to the 1983 *Code*.

5. John Paul II, Apostolic constitution *Sacri canones*, which promulgated the *CCEO*, October 18, 1990, seventh paragraph.

6. The scope of this proliferation is considerable. Volume VIII of *Leges Ecclesiae post Codicem Iuris Canonici Editae* was published in 1998 (Rome: EDIURCLA). It contains the "laws" issued by the Pontiff or the Curia in the ten years 1986–95. It is a book of 1,500 double-column pages of fine print containing excerpts from 456 documents. Since its only indices are chronological and alphabetical by incipits, it is nearly inaccessible.

7. As Pope John Paul II did with his Apostolic letter *Ad tuendam fidem* (May 18, 1998) adding new sections to canons 740 and 1371 of the 1983 *Code* and to canons 598 and 1436 of the *CCEO*.

8. Confer *La Synodalite: La participation au gouvernement dans l'Eglise*, two-volume issue of *L'Année Canonique* (1992), the acts of the seventh international congress of Canon Law, Paris, September 1990.

9. *LG* 22; *CIC*, c. 336; *CCEO*, c. 49.

10. *CIC*, cc. 337, 338.

11. *CIC*, cc. 342, 344.

12. *CIC*, c. 343.

13. Recall the title of John Gratian's epoch-making collection: *Concordia Discordantium Canonum* ("a harmony of discordant canons"; ca. 1140).

14. Gal 2, Acts 15.

15. Confer chapter 7 above on the evolution of ministries.

16. Confer the discussion of inculturation above in chapter 5.

17. More than twenty such regional synods were held in the fourth century alone, in places like Carthage, Arles, and Toledo.

18. The provincial and plenary councils of Baltimore bear ample witness to the enduring effectiveness and influence of conciliar activity in the United States throughout the nineteenth century.

19. *CIC* cc. 439, 446.

20. Confer *CIC* c. 455. The 1983 *Code* requires or allows episcopal conferences to make applications of general norms to the churches of their conference. These "complementary norms" or "particular legislation" are called for in forty-three specific instances. Confer J. T. Martín de Agar, *Legislazione delle Conferenze Episcopali Complementare al C.I.C.* (Milano: Giuffrè, 1990).

21. *CIC*, c. 455.2.

22. Synods assembled in special session, *CIC*, c. 345.

23. *CIC*, c. 343.

24. *UR*, 1.

25. *CIC*, c. 209.1.

26. *Procedural Norms for the Processing of Formal Marriage Cases* (Washington, D.C.: NCCB, 1970), norms 3 and 23.

27. C. J. van der Poel, "Influences of an 'Annulment Mentality,'" *Jurist* 40 (1980): 385.

28. Source: *Annuarium Statisticum Ecclesiae*. To put these U.S. numbers of annulments into perspective, the number of decisions reached in 1985 in all of Europe was 8,683; in all of Africa, 238; in all of

South America, 972. In 1995 those three numbers were reported to be 10,251, 488, and 1,997, respectively.

29. *CIC*, c.1446.1; *CCEO*, c. 1103.1.

30. "If anyone wants to go to law over your shirt, hand him your coat as well" (Mt 5, 40); "When you stand to pray, forgive anyone against whom you have a grievance so that your heavenly Father may in turn forgive you your faults" (Mk 11, 25); "Forgive us the wrong we have done as we forgive those who wrong us" (Mt 6, 14); "If your brother or sister should commit some wrong against you, go and point out his fault, but keep it between the two of you" (Mt 18, 15).

31. For example, a presbyter, deacon, or other skilled person acting in the name of the local church.

32. John Paul II, Apostolic exhortation *Familiaris Consortio*, December 15, 1981, par. 82 (*AAS* 74 [1982]: 183; *On Family Life* [Washington, D.C.: USCC, 1982], 81).

33. *CIC* c. 915; *CCEO* c. 712: "those who are publicly unworthy are forbidden from receiving."

34. "...*salva iustitia*...," *CIC*, c. 1446.1. In a talk to American bishops on the ways that the church approaches declarations of nullity Pope John Paul II said, "The referral of matrimonial cases to the tribunal should be a last resort." October 11, 1998, *Newsletter, Canadian Canon Law Society* 23 (Fall 1998): 16.

BIBLIOGRAPHY

THIS BIBLIOGRAPHY IS INTENDED to assist the reader in locating the sources of the main themes of the book and to pursue further research along the same lines. It does not contain every resource cited in the footnotes. It is divided into three sections:

On the Nature of Canon Law
On the Theology of the Church and Its Ministries
On the History of Canon Law

ON THE NATURE OF CANON LAW

Arrieta, Juan Ignacio. "El pueblo de Dios." *Manual de Derecho Canónico*. Pamplona: EUNSA, 1988. Pp. 113–50.

Aymans, Winfried. "Ekklesiologische Leitlinien in den Entwürfen für dei neue Gesetzgebung." *Theologisches Jarhbuch* (1984): 300–25.

Barrett, Richard. "Canon Law or Canonical Theology? What Does a Theology of Law Mean for the Specificity of Canon Law?" *Irish Theological Quarterly* 60 (1994): 17–38.

Beal, John. "The Exercise of the Power of Governance by Lay People: State of the Question." *Jurist* 55 (1995): 1–92.

Berlingò, Salvatore. "Riflessi del Codice 1983 sulla Dottrina: per una chiave di lettura della canonistica postcodiciale." *Ius Ecclesiae* 6 (1994): 41–90.

Bertolino, Rinaldo. "'Sensus Fidei,' Carismi e Diritto nel Populo di Dio." *Ius Ecclesiae* 7 (1995): 155–98.

———. "Diritto Canonico e Comunione Ecclesiale." *Il Diritto Ecclesiastico* 103 (1992): 137–57.

Bertrams, Wilhelm. "De Natura Iuris Ecclesiae Proprii Notanda." *Periodica* 66 (1977): 567–82.

Beyer, Jean. *Du concile au Code de Droit Canonique: La mise en application de Vatican II*. Paris, 1985.

Bidagor, Raimundo. "El espíritu del Derecho canónico." *Revista Española de Derecho Canonico* 13 (1958): 5–30.

Blanco Fernández, Maria. "Ordenamiento Canonico y Ciencia Juridica con occasion de Nuevas Aportaciones Doctrinales." *Ius Canonicum* 30 (1990): 305–27.

Bonnet, Piero Antonio. "Carità e diritto: la dimensione communitaria quale momento della struttura interna del diritto della Chiesa." *Investigationes theologico-canonicae*. Roma, 1978.

———. "La ministerialitá laicale." *Teologia e Diritto canonico*. Città del Vaticano: Ed. Vaticana, 1987. Pp. 87–130.

Caprile, Giovanni. "Importanza e funzione del diritto canonico." *La Civiltà Cattolica* 128 (1977): II, 176–80.

Cattaneo, Arturo. *Questioni fondamentali della canonistica nel pensiero di Klaus Mörsdorf*. Pamplona: EUNSA, 1986.

———. "Theologia e Diritto nella Definizione Epistmologica della Canonistica." *Ius Ecclesiae* 6 (1994): 649–71.

———. "Teologicidad y Juridicidad de la Canonistica." *Revista Española de Derecho Canonico* 51 (1994): 35–49.

———. "El Debate Científico en torno a la Síntesis Theológico-Jurídica de la Canonística Propuesta por Mörsdorf y su Escuela." *Revista Española de Derecho Canonico* 52 (1995): 81–98.

Celeghin, Adriano. "Sacra Potestas: Quaestio post Conciliaris." *Periodica* 74 (1985): 165–25.

Coccopalmerio, Francesco. "De Conceptu et Natura Iuris Ecclesiae: Animadversiones Quaedam." *Periodica* 66 (1977): 447–74.

———. "Che cose è il diritto della chiesa?" *Perché Un Codice nella Chiesa*. Ed. A. Longhitano. Bologna: Ed. Dehoniane, 1984. Pp. 17–55.

Composta, Dario. *La Chiesa visibile. La realtà de teologia del Diritto canonico*. Città del Vaticano: Typis Poligl. Vaticanis, 1985.

Congar, Yves. "Rudolph Sohm nous interroge encore." *Revue des Sciences Philosophiques et Théologiques* 57 (1973): 263–87.

Corecco, Eugenio. *The Theology of Canon Law: A Methodological Question.* Pittsburgh: Duquesne University Press, 1992.

————. *Ius et Communio: Scritti di Diritto Canonico.* Ed. G. Borgonovo and A. Catteneo. Monferrato: Ed. Piemme, 1997.

D'Avack, Pietro Agostino. *Trattato di diritto canonico. Introduzione sistemica generale.* Milano, 1980.

————. "Legittimità, contenuto e metodologia del diritto canonico." *Il Diritto ecclesiastico e Rassegna di diritto matrimoniale* 89 (1978): I,3–41.

de la Hera, Alberto. "Liquet Ius Canonicum Esse Ius Sacrum Prorsus Distinctum a Iure Civili." *Periodica* 66 (1977): 475–97.

Del Giudice, Vincenzo. *Nozioni di Diritto Canonico.* Milano, 1970.

Demmer, Klaus. "Ius ecclesiae–Ius gratiae: Animadversiones ad Relationem inter Ius Canonicum et Ethos Christianum." *Periodica* 66 (1977): 5–46.

De Paolis, Velasio. "Ius: notio univoca an analoga?" *Periodica* 69 (1980): 127–62.

————. "Communio in novo Codice." *Periodica* 77 (1988): 521–52.

Erdö, Péter. "Law and the Theological Reality of the Church." *Jurist* 56 (1996): 128–60.

Fedele, Pío. *Discorso Generale sull' ordinamento canonico.* Padova: Cedam, 1941.

————. *Lo spirito del diritto canonico.* Roma, 1962.

————. *Discorsi sul diritto canonico.* Roma, 1973.

————. "Utrum Definiri Possit Lex Ecclesiastica Ex Ordine Ad Bonum Commune." *Periodica* 66 (1977): 549–60.

————. "La norma suprema fondamentale dell' ordinamento canonico." *Ephemerides Iurs Canonici* 34 (1978): 191–210.

Fornés, Juan. *La ciencia canónica contemporánea.* Pamplona: EUNSA, 1984.

Fransen, Gérard. "De Analogia Legis Apud Canonistas." *Periodica* 66 (1977): 535–47.

Geroso, Libero. *Diritto Ecclesiale e Pastorale.* Torino: Giappichelli, 1990.

————. *Carisma e Diritto nella Chiesa.* Milano: Ed. Jaca, 1989.

Ghirlanda, Gianfranco. *Il diritto nella Chiesa mistero di communione: Compendio di diritto ecclesiale.* Roma: Ed. Paoline, 1990.

————. *Introduzione al Diritto Ecclesiale*. Monferrato: Piemme, 1993.

————. "De Caritate Ut Elemento Iuridico Fundamentali Constitutivo Iuris Ecclesialis." *Periodica* 66 (1977): 621–55.

————. "De natura, origine et exercitio potestatis regiminis iuxta novum Codicem." *Periodica* 74 (1985):165–225.

Giacchi, Orio. "Innovazione e tradizione nella Chiesa dopo il Concilio." *Ephemerides Iuris Canonici* 26 (1970): 9–24.

————. "La norma nel diritto canonico." *Ephemerides Iuris Canonici* 33 (1977): 7–22.

Gismondi, Pietro. *Il diritto della chiesa dopo il Concilio*. Milano, 1973.

Herranz Casado, Julián. "Renewal and Effectiveness in Canon Law." *Studia Canonica* 28 (1994): 5–31.

————. *Studi sulla nuova legislazione della Chiesa*. Milano: Giuffrè, 1990.

Hervada Xiberta, Javier. *El Derecho del Peublo de Dios, I, Introducción* (with Pedro Lombardía). Pamplona: 1970. This thematic piece was republished as a prolegomenon to the *Commentario Exegético al Código de Derecho Canónico*. Pamplona: EUNSA, 1996. I, 33–155.

————. "Las raices sacramentales del Derecho canonico." *Sacramentalidad de la Iglesia y los Sacramentos*. Pamplona, 1983. Pp. 359–85.

————. *Elementos de Derecho constitucional canónico*. Pamplona, 1987.

————. *Coloquios propedéuticos de Derecho Canónico*. Pamplona, 1990.

Huizing, Peter. "Reflections on the System of Canon Law." *Jurist* 42 (1982): 239–76.

————. "The Sacramental Structure of Church Order and Its Implications." *Jurist* 32 (1972): 479–93.

————. "The Reform of Canon Law." *Concilium* 8 (1965): 95–128.

Jacobs, Ann. "Théologie et droit canonique–Théologie du droit canonique: Quelques ouvrages récents." *Revue théologique de Louvain* 25 (1994): 204–26.

Jiménez Urresti, Teodoro. *De La Teología A La Canonística*. Salamanca: Pub. Univ. Pont. Salamanca, 1993. (Contains an excellent bibliography.)

Koury, Joseph. "*Ius Divinum* as a Canonical Problem: On the Interaction of Divine and Ecclesiastical Laws." *Jurist* 53 (1993): 104–31.

Lejeune, Michel. "Le droit canonique: règle de droit ou règle d'Église?" *Studia Canonica* 23 (1989): 27–38.

————. "Demythologizing Canon Law." *Studia Canonica* 21 (1987): 5–17.

Lombardía, Pedro. *Escritos de Derecho Canónico.* 3 vols. Pamplona, 1973–74.

————. *Lecciones de Derecho canónico.* Madrid, 1984.

————. "Codificación y ordinamiento canónico." *Raccolta di scritti in onore di Pio Fedele.* Perugia, 1984.

————. *El Derecho del Pueblo de Dios* (with Javier Hervada; see entry at his name).

Longhitano, Adolfo. "La dimensione instituzionale della Chiesa sacramento de salvezza." *Il diritto nel mistero della Chiesa, I, Introduzione.* Roma, 1979. Pp. 39–67.

Mörsdorf, Klaus. *Schriften zum kanonischen Recht.* Ed. W. Aymans, K.-T. Geringer, H. Schmitz. Paderborn: Schöningh, 1989.

Müller, Hubert. "De Analogia Verbum Incarnatum inter et Ecclesiam (L.G. 8a)." *Periodica* 66 (1977): 499–512.

————. "Utrum 'Communio' sit principium formale-canonicum novae codificationis Iuris canonicae Ecclesiae Latinae?" *Periodica* 74 (1985): 85–108.

Örsy, Ladislas. *Theology and Canon Law: New Hoizons for Legislation and Interpretation.* Collegeville, Minn.: Liturgical Press, 1992.

————. "Corecco's Theory of Canon Law: A Critical Appraisal." *Jurist* 53 (1993): 186–98.

Pree, Helmuth. "*Ius Divinum* Between Normative Text, Normative Content, and Material Value Structure." *Jurist* 56 (1996): 41–67.

Redaelli, Carlo. *Il concetto di Diritto della Chiesa nella Riflessione canonistica tra Concilio e Codice.* Milano: Ed. Glossa, 1991. (Contains a fine bibliography.)

————. "La canonistica nel contesto delle scienze teologiche." *Quaderni di diritto ecclesiale* 10 (1997): 28–39.

Rouco Varela, Antonio Maria. "El Derecho Canónico al servicio de la comunión eclesial." *Ius in Vita et in Missione Ecclesiae.* Pont. Council on Interpretation of Legal Texts (Acts of the Symposium held at the Vatican on the tenth anniversary of the promulgation of the 1983 *Code*, April 19–14, 1993),133–53.

————. "Le statut ontologique et epistomologique du droit canonique. Notes pour une théologie du droit canonique." *Revue des Sciences Philosophiques et Théologiques* 57 (1973): 203–27.

Sobanski, Remigiusz. "De Theologicis et Sociologicis Praemissis Theoriae Iuris Ecclesialis Elaborandae." *Periodica* 66 (1977): 657–81.

―――. "L'ecclésiologie du nouveau *Code de Droit Canonique*." *The New Code of Canon Law* (Proceedings of the 5th International Congress of Canon Law), I, 247–70. Ottawa: Saint Paul University, 1986.

―――. "De constitutione ecclesiae et natura iuris in mysterio divino intelligendis." *Monitor Ecclesiasticus* 100 (1975): 268–94.

―――. *Grundlagenproblematik des katholischen Kirchenrechts*. Wien: Böhlau, 1987.

Sohm, Rudolph. *Kirchenrecht, I: die geschichtlichen Grundlagen*. Leipzig, 1892; Berlin, 1970.

La Synodalité: La participation au gouvernement dans l'Église. Actes du VIIe congrès international de Droit canonique, Paris, 1990. Special two-volume edition of *L'année Canonique*. Paris: Éd. Letouzay et Ané, 1992.

Teologia e diritto canonico. Città del Vaticano: Editrice Vaticano, 1987.

Urrutia, Francisco Javier. "De natura legis ecclesiasticae." *Monitor Ecclesiasticus* 100 (1975): 400–419.

―――. "Legis ecclesiasticae definitio." *Periodica* 75 (1986): 303–35.

Vera Urbano, Francisco. "De Natura Iuris Canonici." *Periodica* 66 (1977): 693–704.

Viladrich Bataller, Pedro-Juan. "Hacia una teoría fundamental del Derecho canónico." *Ius Canonicum* 10 (1970): 5–66.

―――. "Derecho y pastoral—La Justicia y la función del Derecho canónico en la edificación de la Iglesia." *Ius Canonicum* 13 (1973): 171–256.

―――. "El 'ius divinum' como creiterio de autenticidad en el Derecho de la Iglesia." *Ius Canonicum* 16 (1976): 91–144.

Walf, Knut. *Einführung in das neue katholische Kirchenrecht*. Köln: Benziger, 1984.

Wijlens, Myriam. *Theology and Canon Law: The Theories of Klaus Mörsdorf and Eugenio Corecco*. Lanham, Md.: University of America Press, 1992.

―――. "The Church Knowing and Acting: The Relationship between Theology and Canon Law." *Louvain Studies* 20 (1995): 21–40.

―――. "Values and Canon Law." *Louvain Studies* 20 (1995): 393–400.

ON THE THEOLOGY OF THE CHURCH AND ITS MINISTRIES

Alberigo, Giuseppe. "The Authority of the Church in the Documents of Vatican I and Vatican II." *Journal of Ecumenical Studies* 19 (1982): 119–45.

Anglican-Roman Catholic International Commission. "Authority in the Church, I." Agreed Statement. Venice, 1976. "Elucidation." "Authority in the Church, II." Windsor, 1981. *The Final Report,* 47–98. Washington, D.C.: USCC, 1982.

Colombo, Giuseppe. "La teologia della Chiesa locale." *La teologia della Chiesa locale.* Ed.: A. Tessarolo. Bologna: Dehoniane, 1969. Pp. 17–38.

————. "Il 'Populo di Dio' e il 'mistero' della Chiesa nell' ecclesiologia post-conciliare." *Teologia* 10 (1985): 97–169.

Congar, Yves. *Vraie et Fausse Réforme dans L'Église.* Paris: Éd. du Cerf, 1968.

————. "De la communion des Églises à une ecclésiologie de l'Église universelle." *L'Épiscopat et L'Église Universelle.* Ed. Y. Congar and B.-D. Dupuy. Paris: Éd. Du Cerf, 1962. Pp. 227–60.

————. *L'Église: Une, Sainte, Catholique et Apostolique.* Paris: Cerf, 1970.

————. "Autonomie et pouvoir central dans l'Église vus après la théologie catholique." *Irenikon* 53 (1980): 291–313.

————. *I Believe in the Holy Spirit.* 3 vols. New York: Seabury, 1983.

————. *Droit ancien et structures ecclésiales.* A collection of previously published articles. London: Variorum Reprints, 1982.

Congregation of the Doctrine of the Faith. Letter, May 28, 1992. "On Some Aspects of the Church Understood as Communion (*Communionis notio*)." *AAS* 85 (1993): 838–50. *Origins* 22:7 (June 25, 1992): 108–12.

Cunningham, Agnes. "Power and Authority in the Church." *The Ministry of Governance.* Ed. J. Mallett. Washington, D.C.: Canon Law Society of America, 1986. Pp. 80–97.

Dianich, Severino. *La Chiesa Mistero di Comunione.* Genova: Marietti, 1987.

————. *Chiesa estroversa: Una ricerca sulla svolta dell' ecclesiologia contemporanea.* Milano: Pioline, 1987.

Fahey, Michael. "Church." *Systematic Theology: Jesus and the Church.* Ed. F. Fiorenza and J. Galvin. Minneapolis: Fortress, 1991. II, 3–74.

Fiorenza, Francis Schüssler. *Foundational Theology: Jesus and the Church*. New York: Crossroad, 1984.

Fransen, Piet. "The Exercise of Authority in the Church Today: Its Concrete Forms." *Louvain Studies* 9 (1982–83): 1–25.

————. "Criticism of Some Basic Theological Notions in Matters of Church Authority." *Journal of Ecumenical Studies* 19 (1982): 48–74.

————, ed. *Authority in the Church*. Articles which appeared in the *Journal of Ecumenical Studies* 19 (1982). Leuven: University Press, 1983.

Hamer, Jerome. *The Church Is a Communion*. New York: Sheed & Ward, 1964.

Hertling, Ludwig. *Communio: Church and Papacy in Early Christianity*. Chicago: Loyola University Press, 1972.

International Theological Commission. "Select Themes of Ecclesiology." *International Theological Commission: Texts and Documents, 1969–1985*. Ed. M. Sharkey. San Francisco: Ignatius Press, 1989. Pp. 267–304.

Kasper, Walter. *Theology and Church*. New York: Crossroad, 1989.

Kilmartin, Edward. *Christian Liturgy: Theology and Practice*. Kansas City: Sheed & Ward, 1988.

————. "Lay Participation in the Apostolate of the Hierarchy." *Jurist* 41 (1981): 343–70.

Komonchak, Joseph. "Subsidiarity in the Church: The State of the Question." *Jurist* 48 (1988): 298–349.

————. "Concepts of Communion. Past and Present." *Cristianesimo nella storia* 16 (1995): 321–40.

————. "The Local Church and the Church Catholic: The Contemporary Theological Problematic." *Jurist* 52 (1992): 416–47.

————. "The Synod of 1985 and the Notion of Church." *Chicago Studies* 28 (1987): 330–45.

————. "The Theological Debate." *Synod 1985–An Evaluation (Concilium*, 188). Ed. G. Alberigo and J. Provost. Edinburgh: Clark, 1986. Pp. 53–63.

Legrand, Hervé. "La Réalisation de L'Église en un Lieu." *Initiation à la Practique de la Théologie*. Ed. B. Lauret and F. Refoulé, III. Paris: Ed. Du Cerf, 1986. Dogmatique 2, 143–273, 331–43.

Lennan, Richard. *The Ecclesiology of Karl Rahner*. New York: Oxford University Press, 1995.

Leys, Ad. *Ecclesiological Impacts of the Principle of Subsidiarity*. Tiburg: Kok-Kampen, 1995.

MacDonald, Timothy. *The Ecclesiology of Yves Congar: Foundational Themes*. Lanham, Md.: University Press, 1984.

Nichols, Aidan. *Yves Congar*. London: Geoffrey Chapman, 1989.

O'Donnell, Christopher. *Ecclesia: A Theological Encyclopedia of the Church*. Collegeville, Minn.: Liturgical Press, 1996.

O'Meara, Thomas. *Theology of Ministry*. Rev. ed. New York: Paulist, 1999.

Osborne, Kenan. *Priesthood: A History of Ordained Ministry in the Roman Catholic Church*. New York: Paulist, 1988.

——————. *Ministry: Lay Ministry in the Roman Catholic Church: Its History and Theology*. New York: Paulist, 1993.

Power, David. *Gifts That Differ: Lay Ministries Established and Unestablished*. New York: Pueblo, 1980.

Provost, James, and Walf, Knut, eds. *Power in the Church (Concilium, 197)*. Edinburgh: Clark, 1988.

Rahner, Karl. *Concern for the Church (Theological Investigations, XX)*. New York: Crossroads, 1981.

Rausch, Thomas. *Authority and Leadership in the Church: Past Directions and Future Possibilities*. Wilmington: Glazier, 1989.

Routhier, Gilles. "La synodalité de l'Église locale." *Studia Canonica* 26 (1992): 111–61.

——————. "'Église locale' ou 'Église particulière': querelle sémantique ou option théologique?" *Studia Canonica* 25 (1991): 277–334.

Schillebeeckx, Edward. *Church: The Human Story of God*. New York: Crossroad, 1990.

——————. *The Mission of the Church*. New York: Seabury, 1973.

——————. *The Church with a Human Face: A New and Expanded Theology of Ministry*. New York: Crossroad,1988.

Sullivan, Francis. *The Church We Believe In: One, Holy, Catholic and Apostolic*. New York: Paulist, 1988.

Tillard, Jean-Marie. *Church of Churches: The Ecclesiology of Communion*. Collegeville, Minn.: Liturgical Press, 1992.

——————. "Autorité et memoire dans l'Église." *Irenikon* 61 (1988): 332–46, 481–84.

Walsh, Michael, and Davies, Brian. *Proclaiming Justice & Peace: Papal Documents from Rerum Novarum through Centesimus Annus*. Mystic, Conn.: Twenty-Third Publications, 1991.

ON THE HISTORY OF CANON LAW:

Cicognani, Amleto G. *Canon Law*. Philadelphia: Dolphin, 1935. Pp. 131–412.

Coussa, Acacius. *Epitome Praelectionum de Iure Ecclesiastico Orientali, I*. Grottoferrata, 1948.

Dictionnaire de Droit Canonique. Ed. R. Naz. 7 vols. Paris: Letouzey et Anè, 1935–65. (Nearly every entry includes a historical perspective.)

Erdö, Péter. *Introductio in Historiam Scientiae Canonica*. Roma: Ed. Pont. Univ. Gregoriana, 1990.

Feine, Hans. *Kirchliche Rechtsgeschicte Der katholische Kirche*. 5th ed. Köln: Bohlau, 1972.

García y García, Antonio. *Historia del derecho canónico, I, Il primo Milenio*. Salamanca, 1967.

Gaudemet, Jean. *Storia del Diritto Canonico: Ecclesia et Civitas*. Milano: Edizioni San Paulo, 1998. (A translation of *Église et Cité. Histoire du droit canonique*. Paris: Cerf, 1994.)

Giacobbi, A. "Il diritto nella storia della Chiesa. Sintesi di storia delle fonte e delle instituzioni." *Il Diritto nel mistero della Chiesa, I*. Rome, 1979. Pp. 117–236.

Hervada, Javier y Lombardía, Pedro. "El Drecho Canónico en la Historia." *El Derecho del Pueblo de Dios, I, Introducción*. Pamplona, 1970. Republished as a prolegomenon to *Commentario Exegético al Códico de Derecho Canónico*. 8 vols. Pamplona: EUNSA, 1996. I, 91–155.

Kurtscheid, P. Bertrandus. *Historia Iuris Canonici: Historia Institutorum ab Ecclesiae Fundatione usque ad Gratianum*. Roma: Catholic Book Agency, 1951.

Le Bras, Gabriel et Gaudemet, Jean, eds. *Histoire du Droit et des Institutions de l'Église en Occident*. 16 vols. Paris: Sirey (later Cujas), 1955–81.

Musselli, L. *Storia del diritto canonico*. Torino, 1992.

Plöchl, Willibald. *Geschicte des Kirchenrichts*. 2nd ed. 3 vols. Wien: Herold, 1958–66. (Italian translation, in two vols., Milano, 1963.)

Salachas, Dimitrios. *Instituzioni di Diritto Canonico delle Chiese Catoliche Orientali*. Roma: Dehoniane, 1993. Part I.

Stickler, Alphonsus. *Historia Iuris Canonici Latini, I, Historia Fontium*. Torino: Pont. Athenaeum Salesiani, 1950.

Tejero, Eloy. "Formacion Historica del Derecho Canónico." *Manual de Derecho Canónico*. 2nd ed. Pamplona: EUNSA, 1991. Pp. 51–111.

Van De Wiel, Constant. *History of Canon Law*. Louvain: Peeters, 1991.

Van Hove, A. *Prolegomena ad Codicem Iuris Canonici*. 2nd ed. Malines: Dessain, 1945. (An especially rich bibliographical source.)

Zeiger, Ivo. *Historia Iuris Canonici, I, De Historia Fontium et Scientiae Iuris Canonici*. Roma: Univ. Gregoriana, 1947.

INDEX

Abelard, Peter, 144
academic abstractness, 7–8
Acts of the Apostles, 57, 92
Adrian I, pope of Rome, 30
aggiornamento, 8, 160
"altar communities," 35
American Association of Retired
    Persons, 36
"American Norms," 168
Ananias, 49
Antioch, 22, 44, 82
Apostolic Constitution on Fast
    and Abstinence, 89
apostolicity, 56–58
Aquila, 134
Aquinas, Thomas, 15, 121,
    142
Areopagus, 120
auctoritas, 107
Augustine, Saint, 44, 115, 143

baptism, 17, 44
Barnabas, 22
Bertrams, William, 9

Bishop's Committee for
    Canonical Affairs, 167
Bonhoeffer, Dietrich, 12

canon, 27
Canon Law, 16–17, 19–20, 31–32,
    125–26, 132–33, 139–41,
    151–52, 159, 172–73. *See
    also* canonical ministry;
    canonists
causes of debate on nature
    of, 7–8, 13; code revision
    process, 8–9, 159–63;
    negative image, 10–11;
    Sohm's accusation, 11
definition, 1–2
and diversity of discipline,
    163–67; and regional
    councils, 165–66, 186nn.
    17, 18
English, 28, 175n. 4
nature of, 11–13, 31, 132
and power language, 107
relation to other disciplines,
    139; church history,

141–42; ecclesiology, 144–45; moral theology, 145–46; sacred scripture, 139–41; theology, 142–44 relation to other ministries, 146–47, 149–50; administration, 149; catechesis, 147; liturgical celebration, 148; pastoral counseling, 148; preaching, 147 schools of thought on nature of, 13, 19–20, 174n. 6; Concilium Project, 18–19, 175n. 12, 184n. 18; institutional school, 18–19, 175n. 15, 184n. 19; Munich school, 14–16, 175n. 10, 184n. 22; Opus Dei school, 12, 14; public ecclesiastical law school, 13–14; Roman curia school, 16, 175n. 11, 184n. 18; school of values, 17–18 as a science, 150; and divine law, 150–51; juridical, 152–53; as theological discipline, 151–52

Canon Law Society of America, 167, 182n. 1

canonical creativity, 167–72

canonical ministry, 1–3, 20, 32, 33–34, 106–7, 131, 172. *See also* Canon Law, relation to other ministries; canonists; Christian freedom; church; church authority; churches in place

and change, 136–39 definition, 135–36 education for, 154–57 future, 159. *See also* canonical revision and gift of good guidance, 134–35 hazards of according to Jesus, 157–58 New Testament rules, 21, 26–27; conflict resolution, 23–24; decision-making, 22–23; qualifications for leaders, 25–27; use of spiritual gifts, 24–25

canonical revision, 159–63

canonico, 28

canonique, 28

canonists, 2, 3–4, 9, 12, 65–66, 70, 78, 79–80, 132–33, 140, 153, 167, 182nn. 2, 3. *See also* canonical ministry; Christian freedom; church; church authority; churches in place

capitula, 30

Cassian, John, 93

catholicism, 37

Celestial Hierarchy, The (Pseudo-Dionysius), 121

charismata, 24–25, 41. *See also* Holy Spirit, gifts of

Christian freedom, 79–80, 104–5, 178n. 4 in Christ, 80–83 and discernment of the Spirit, 91–95 and personal conscience, 86–89

and power of discretion,
89–91
and religious freedom,
83–86
and rights of persons and
communities, 95–100;
community rights,
98–99, 179n. 19;
individual Catholic
rights, 96–97
Christianity and Roman law, 115
church, 5, 17, 60. *See also* church
authority; churches in
place; "proprietary
churches"
apostolic nature, 56–59
as body of Christ, 52–53
as communion of
communions, 99–100
as community of word and
sacrament, 15, 37–38
history, 28–29, 115–18,
141–42; authority of
concordats, 30–31; and
Charlemagne, 29–30;
Christian emperors, 29;
concordat with
Napoleon, 31; papal class
on secular power, 30
local, 34–38, 51–52, 53, 56,
59, 61–63, 66–68, 72, 74,
78, 89, 103–4, 149, 152,
171, 172–73
mission, 50–52
missionary efforts, 100,
163–64
and people of God concept,
48–50
as sacrament of salvation,
17, 53–56

unity, 59–60, 166
as voluntary association,
102–3
church authority, 106–7, 130–31.
See also Second Vatican
Council, on church
authority
distortions of, 114–18
and laypersons, 125–30
monarchical, 125, 181n. 22
participative, 122–25
scope of Christ's authority,
109–11
as service, 111–14
sources of power, 107–9
churches in place
elements, 74;
economic conditions,
66–69; education, 72–73;
employment, 73–74;
ethnicity and race,
64–65; geographic
location, 70–71; history,
71–72; language, 63;
political systems, 65–66;
religious context, 69–70
principles, 75, 78;
solidarity, 76–77;
subsidiarity, 75–76
Climacus, John, 93
Code of Canon Law (1917), 9, 155,
160, 161, 167–68
Code of Canon Law (1959), 8, 10
Code of Canon Law (1983), 9, 18,
95–96, 122, 125, 145,
155, 160–61, 168, 180n.
14 and "divine law," 151,
183n. 14

Code of Canons for the Eastern
    Churches (1990), 95–96,
    107, 125, 161
collegiality, 124
Commission for the Revision of
    the Code, 127
communio, 43, 48
communio ecclesialis, 16
communio ecclesiarum, 15, 42–43,
    46
"communio ecclesiology," 10, 17,
    33, 176n. 1
communio fidelium, 40, 42
communio hierarchica, 43, 46
communio sanctorum, 42
communion, 15–16, 41. See also
    Second Vatican Council,
    and components of
    communion
aspects, 43–46
elements, 46–47
meanings, 42–43
communion of churches, 15
Congar, Yves, 11
Congregation for Catholic
    Education, 154
Congregation for the Doctrine of
    the Faith, 127
congrua potestas discretionis, 89, 90
consanguinity, 183n. 14
Constitution on Penance, 90
constitutiones, 29
Council of Jerusalem. See
    Jerusalem, "council of"

Damaris, 120
deacons, 25, 26, 124, 137–38
Declaration on Religious Freedom,
    83–86

Decree on the Ministry and Life of
    Priests, 94
Deus Scientiarum Dominus (1931),
    155
diakonia, 113, 135
diakonoi, 25, 137
diakonos, 112, 113
Dionysian–Hadrian Collection,
    30
Dionysius the Areopagite, 120–21
divorced Catholics. See canonical
    creativity
Dogmatic Constitution on the
    Church (Lumen Gentium),
    10, 39–40, 53–54
doulos, 112
dunamis, 108, 109, 110, 111
dunamis kai exousia, 109–10

ecclesia congregata, 40
Ecclesiastical Hierarchy, The
    (Pseudo-Dionysius),
    121–22
ecclesiology, 14, 33, 144–45
ekklesia, 36
entia rationis, 34
epiclesis, 38
epikeia, 170
Episcopal Synod (1975), 101
Episcopal Synod for Asia (1998),
    102
episkopoi, 25
episkopos, 137
Epistle of James, 82
Eucharist, 17, 37–38, 44–45
    and action of the Holy
    Spirit, 38–41
Eusebius, 121
exousia, 108, 109, 110

factotum, 115
formalism, 156, 161

Germanic property law, 115–16
global communications, 64, 167
Gospel of John, 80, 112
Gospel of Matthew, 23–24, 157

Holy Spirit, 38–41, 43–44, 51, 53,
    91–92, 108–9, 128–29,
    166. *See also* Christian
    freedom, and
    discernment of the Spirit
  gifts of, 24–25, 97, 123,
    134–35, 182n. 4
  presence in church
    community, 62
Huizing, Peter, 9

Ignatius of Loyola, 93
in necesariis, 166
in variis formis . . . disciplinae, 166
inculturation, 100–102
Introduction to Canon Law, An
    (Coriden), 4
iura, 96
ius canonicum, 27, 31
ius civile, 27
ius divinum, 150
ius publicum ecclesiasticum, 14, 153

James, 22
Jerusalem, 22, 44, 49, 68, 136
  "council of," 23, 82–83, 123,
    162
Jesus Christ, 43, 50, 53, 56–57,
    59, 80–82, 91–92, 108–9,
    113, 127–28, 139. *See also*
    canonical ministry,
    hazards of according to

Jesus; church; church
    authority, scope of
    Christ's authority
  on avoiding litigation, 169,
    187n. 30
  compared by Paul to a
    helmsman, 134–35, 182n. 6
  denunciation of scribes and
    Pharisees, 157–58
  and the disciples, 85, 111,
    119–20
  and the Roman centurion,
    119
  sayings of, 169, 187n. 30
juridicism, 155–56
Justinian, 29, 30

kanon, 27
King, Martin Luther, Jr., 12
Kirchenrecht, 28
koinonia, 41, 44
kubernein, 134
kubernesis, 134

laity-hierarchy dualism, 48
"lay investiture controversy," 116,
    180n. 9
laypersons. *See* church authority,
    and laypersons
legalism, 10–11
Leges Ecclesiae post Codicem Iuris
    Canonici Editae (1988),
    185n. 6
lex, 27
lex divina, 151
liberalism, 80
libertas christiana, 80
litterae pacis, 45
liturgy, 38
locus theologicus, 144

Lombardía, Peter, 9
Lonergan, Bernard, 18
Lumen Gentium. See Dogmatic
  Constitution on the
  Church

marriage annulment process,
  167–71
  and number of annulments,
  168, 186–87n. 28
  and tribunal process,
  169–70
mater et magistra, 75
ministerium, 135
ministry. *See* canonical ministry
Mörsdorf, Klaus, 9
Mosaic law, 81, 83, 87
munera, 50
Muslim nations, 69

New Testament, 33, 108, 111
  churches, 44, 163
  sources of power in, 107–9
nomos, 27
novus habitas mentis, 18, 155

ordinatio fidei, 15
ordinatio rationis, 15
Origen, 93

*Pastoral Constitution on the Church
  in the Modern World,* 93
Paul, Saint, the Apostle, 12, 22,
  52, 68, 106, 110, 113,
  134–35
  and Christian vocation,
  81–82
  and Corinth, 130
  on gifts of the Spirit, 24–25
  on the "interior law," 87

Peace of Constantine, 84
Peter, Saint, 22
Philemon, 134
Platonism, 122, 142
Pontifical University of the Holy
  Cross, 14
Pope Benedict XV, 160
Pope Boniface VIII, 30, 116
Pope Gregory VII, 30, 116
Pope Gregory the Great, 121
Pope John XXIII, 8, 75, 160
Pope John Paul II, 75–76, 77, 101,
  120
Pope Martin I, 121
Pope Paul VI, 89–90, 94, 101, 127,
  138, 156, 167, 185n. 36
Pope Pius XI, 75
Pope Pius XII, 127
postmodern challenges to the
  church, 2
potestas, 107
potestas iurisdictionis, 125
potestas regiminis, 125
presbyteroi, 25, 136
Prisca, 134
"proprietary churches," 115–16
Protestant Reformation, 80, 84,
  117
Pseudo-Dionysius, 121

ratio legis, 143
recognitio, 9
regula, 27
Roman Catholic Church, 4, 5, 28,
  43, 83
"Rudolf Sohm Still Questions
  Us," 11

Sacrae disciplinae leges, 180n. 14
sacraments, 17

sacramentum mundi, 152
Saint Mary's of Main Street. *See*
     church, local
salus animarum suprema lex, 13,
     152
Saphira, 49
Sapientia Christiana (1979), 155
Second Vatican Council (Vatican
     II), 3, 18, 31–32, 48, 53,
     80, 86–87, 90, 127–28,
     151, 166. *See also*
     Christian freedom;
     *Declaration on Religious
     Freedom*
   on church authority,
     118–20
   on the College of Bishops,
     143, 162–63
   and components of
     communion, 46–47
   definition of the church,
     35–37
   and the diaconate, 138
   and ecclesiology, 9–10,
     144–45
   and the episcopate, 138
   on marriage, 143
   on priestly formation, 154

   statement on church of
     Christ, 35
Sohm, Rudolf, 11
stabilitas legis, 161–62
status personarum, 169
sui generis, 13
Synod of Bishops (1967), 76, 89,
     162
Synod of Bishops (1974), 95

Theodosius, 29, 30
theology, 16–17, 33–34, 40,
     142–43
   moral, 145–46
Timothy, 57–58
toto caelo, 153

ubi societas ibi ius, 13, 153
Unam Sanctum (1302), 30
unicuique suum, 153
University of Navarra, 14

Vatican II. *See* Second Vatican
     Council
vere adest, 35

Washington Theological Union, 4
"world church," 100, 164